THE SERPENTS OF EDEN

By Andrew Hennessey

CONTENTS

INTRODUCTION - THE HUMAN RACE FOR REALITY.

Over the years since first writing Monkeys of Eden - the Telepathic Overlords and the Slaves of Earth, in 1999, I often regretted penning a somewhat reactive story from the point of view of the 'Monkeys' ..
Since then, I have made other attempts to explain the 'status quo' here - for example; why I think that if humanity ever run out of crude oil, aliens would then manufacture it for our use using free-energy technology in - 'Escape from Earth', and, the mechanism by which the other non-serpentine, but insectoid greys are socially utilised here in a janitorial capacity in 'Harvesting the Disconnected' which perhaps explains 'how' humans are being farmed, plus 'Alien Encounters and the Paranormal' - a recent more textbook-like look into UFOlogy and the folklore both ancient and modern, and 21st Century Space-Age Faerie Tales - which contains some examples of my own 'close encounters' etc

Having felt my first work in 1999AD - 'Monkeys of Eden - the

Telepathic Overlords and the Slaves of Earth' could have been less reactive and more erudite - to come up with a sequel, therefore, would be to address the issues of the planetary Reptilian contingent, but not by using a 'reactive' personal approach or some 'monkey-esque victim mentality'.

Yet, clearly the quality of life for the majority on the planets surface is; unchanging, bizarre and desolate for no good reason.

What better to start a work on the Serpents of Eden then, than with proof that the realm of the Earth's surface has been governed by and basically left with a debilitating 'status quo' for millennia.

The ancient hero Calgacus or the 'swordsman' - can be heard rallying the troops - in the following quote. His large army of hopefuls then promptly gets wiped out by the 9th Roman Legion at the battle of Mons Graupius, North-east Scotland, 84AD.

It's also true that the returning, victorious 9th never made it home - but that's probably another story.

The quote ends with *'.. they make a desert and they call it peace'* statement which sounds basically as true today as it has always been in all previous contests throughout the human millennia. It's as enduring a truth as Tony Blair's *'things can only get better..'* quote, used to get him elected as the UK Prime minister in the 1990's. (20th Century).

Bear in mind that in the 21st Century there are still billions of disadvantaged people under the heel of some legion - and things basically did not get better.
Instead the planet has become an 'unsustainable' and in places toxic desert, and people to people 'the world over', despite all the 'fraternal' machinations are still not part of one big happy family.

In fact, on Earth, its rather like something with an unsatiable lust for desolation and destruction has been giving mostly the Race of Adam a very hard time - all the time.

Who or what are the 'Serpents of Eden' ? how do they operate on Earth, and why ?

This work will look into some of these matters.

After the famous quote from Calgacus - we too will go 'roaming in the gloaming' i.e. wandering the Scottish twilight zone - to see what we can see and then - we'll attempt to draw some conclusions from what we can see or recognise of the timeless modus operandii of the 'Serpents of Eden'.

In the words mainly of Calgacus, Pictish hero (Scotland) in AD84; As recorded by the Roman Historian Tacitus, Agricola (XXXII)

"You have not tasted servitude. There is no land beyond us and even the sea is no safe refuge when we are threatened by the (sic. X, Imperial Rome etc e.g. 'Anunnaki', ed.)....We are the last people on earth, and the last to be free: our very remoteness in a land known only to rumour has protected us up till this day. Today the furthest bounds of Britain lie open and everything unknown is given an inflated worth. But now there is no people beyond us, nothing but tides and rocks and, more deadly than these, the (sic. Romans, X, 'Anunnaki', ed.). It is no use trying to escape their arrogance by submission or good behaviour. They have pillaged the world: when the land has nothing left for men who ravage everything, they scour the sea. If an enemy is rich, they are greedy, if he is poor, they crave glory. Neither East nor West can sate their appetite. They are the only people on earth to covet wealth and poverty with equal craving. They plunder, they butcher, they ravish, and call it by the lying name of 'empire'. They make a desert and call it 'peace'"

There are though, two sides to every story – hence this - a 20-years-after follow-up sequel, to the 'Monkeys of Eden', 1999, 'The Serpents of Eden' in 2019.

I am the very first person to admit to the truth of these matters as it pertains to myself - i.e. The human mind is a flawed and failed artefact that can be very easily diverted and derailed and blanked out by whatever powers and processes exist in this world generally beyond human knowledge.

It was the French philosopher Descartes in the 17th Century who proposed that a human being could not know if their vision of the world and reality was being subsumed by an evil demonic mind – i.e. 'Descartes Demon'.

We do have a prayer though.

This is my disclaimer, therefore, for what I will say in this work - as it is mostly speculation produced by a falsifiable human mind.

For human beings on Earth, souls, that were born as blank slates or *tabula rasa* upon which are to be written what our bretheren experience and also what we are then given the grace to write - must pray to, resonate with and connect to goodness: our one life-line out of this dark maze.

Tabula rasa is a Latin phrase often translated as "clean slate" in English and originates from the Roman tabula used for notes, which was blanked by heating the wax and then smoothing it. This roughly equates to the English term "blank slate" (or, more literally, "erased slate") which refers to the emptiness of a slate prior to it being written on with chalk. Both may be renewed repeatedly, by melting the wax of the tablet or by erasing the chalk on the slate.

Some people on Earth believe that some people have past-life memories that are not falsely implanted by the demonic or zeta reticulan.

Repeatedly recycling soul prisoners from wars as livestock because they have something they want to write, wiping the slate clean so that they can be reborn is an experience of 'Ralph' an ex-CIA Accountant from Canada. [ca. 1980] His last memories were of being an alien pilot in an alien body, betraying his society in an interstellar conflict, then crashing as a WW1 pilot in a German Biplane, then a US Pilot in WW2, and each time he can remember being in a SCI-FI control room above the Earth before being placed into his next incarnation!

Comparison of the mind to a blank writing tablet occurs in Aristotle's De Anima (4th century BC; On the Soul), and the Stoics as well as the Peripatetics (students at the Lyceum, the school founded by Aristotle) subsequently argued for an original state of mental blankness. Both the Aristotelians and the Stoics, however, emphasized those faculties of the mind or soul that, having been only potential or inactive before receiving ideas from the senses, respond to the ideas by an intellectual process and convert them into knowledge.

A new and revolutionary emphasis on the tabula rasa occurred late in the 17th century, when the English empiricist John Locke, in An Essay Concerning Human Understanding (1689), argued for the mind's initial resemblance to "white paper, void of all characters," with "all the materials of reason and knowledge" derived from experience.

Writer Andrew Hennessey argues in his work 'Tripartite Essentialsm' for a human mind derivable from such stimulus, defining the interactive process by which stimulus creates mind.

That is not to argue against 'innate' mind which can be clearly heard and sometimes seen on e.g. youtubes by the very very young and gifted easily cutting out decades and decibels of the trial and error of human learning and angst.

The blank human being has no real or innate sense of history, or memory, or recall or the sophistry produced by high levels of multitasking and multiprocessing.

Whatever it is that causes, maintains and polices such toxic grief on Earth by its nature, is not really anchored in the same time-space as its Race-of-Adam flocks.Whether Reptilian or Demonic, however masquerading:- its husbandry or shepherding behaviour will have a biological model or analogy.

For example, Symbiosis is an umbrella term referring to any long-term interaction between two organisms that share a close physical space. Symbiosis is broken down into mutualism, commensalism, and parasitism based on how two species interact in their ecosystem. Mutualism is where both organisms benefit, commensalism is where one benefits but the other organism isn't harmed, and lastly, parasitism is where one organism benefits and the other is harmed. [www. sciencetrends .com]

Race of Adam - human souls - engage in outward-looking social constructionism, from; cave art to logistics, from irrigation to AI. They live within the constraints and blinkers of 'Plato's Cave', and therefore, naturally, extend out into and amongst the shadows. Their vision and expectation of social outcomes is also so constrained.

Adamic humans tend to be slow and sluggish in their movements and thoughts, and have usually little capacity to use tools and process data at great speeds.

What if, though, there are beings on Earth - call them 'Ultraterrestrial' or 'interdimensional' *[i.e. Ultraterrestrials are beings who come from beyond the realm of human experience altogether, whether from a parallel universe, alternate dimension, or another space time continuum]* .. whose presence amongst the humans inside the darkness of the cave was not limited by such things that slow ordinary tabula rasa humans down. Not limited by time-space, they could literally run rings around us.

The Allegory of the Cave, or Plato's Cave, was presented by the Greek philosopher Plato in his work Republic (514a–520a) to compare *"the effect of education and the lack of it on our nature"*.

Plato has Socrates describe a group of people who have lived chained to the wall of a cave all of their lives, facing a blank wall. The people watch shadows projected on the wall from objects passing in front of a fire/light behind them, and then give names to these shadows. The shadows are the prisoners' reality. The communal reality is made out of social constructs.

Socrates explains that the philosopher is like a prisoner who is freed from the cave and comes to understand that the shadows on the wall are not reality at all, for he can perceive the true form of [Ultra Terrestrial] reality rather than the manufactured reality that is the shadows seen by the prisoners. The inmates of this place do not even desire to leave their prison, for they know no better life. The prisoners manage to break their bonds one day, and discover that their reality was not what they thought it was. They discovered the sun, which Plato uses as an analogy for the fire that [Adamic] man cannot see behind.

Unlike the eternal fire that cast light on the walls of the cave, the human condition, though, and its souls, are temporarily disorientated and bound to the impressions that are received through the senses. Even if these interpretations are an absurd misrepresentation of the eternal reality, we cannot somehow collectively break free from the bonds of our human condition —we cannot free ourselves from phenomenal state just as the prisoners could not free themselves from their chains.

If, however, we were to miraculously recognise our true bondage to images of self, and then escape our bondage, we would - according to Plato, find a world, a higher reality, that we could not understand—the sun is incomprehensible for someone who has never seen it, but then - one can equally argue that for God, nothing is impossible.

If though such bright futures and luminous events can be perceived with the heart and soul, then, recognition of the big picture of eternally sustaining nurture and truth becomes more instantaneous than attempting to directly and humanly focus on process, verify and recognise every detail and its relationships with the artificial and easily distorted mind or *'nous'*.

For example, every bit of cell biology that lives, gives the water of life to its neighbours, maintains itself and draws nourishment from its Source. (This was and is Christ's New Covenant)

Recognition of the most simple natural analogy about how life lives, loves and eternally persists amongst chaos, confusion and distress, is a great and unending gift to the Race of Adam.

Yet, Human skills on Earth are either tediously hard won - or graced by good, or are a quick, self-negating hook into evil and the sewers of death where their *'worm does not die, nor their fires go out'*.

Relatively speaking the average human being tends to be a bit retarded in the applications department even though they require lots of rationality to deduce the truth behind the social paradoxes and surreal conundrums that they come across. Relatively speaking some people on Earth tend to be operating massive mainframes and high-end software on space age broadband whilst the average human tends to be operating a clunky 486 with freeware and windows95.

It's not that I am not or could not, ever be as good as, beings that can sublimely multitask at levels of genius that a genetically 'ordinary' being may find challenging, but then there is us - the 'ordinary' *tabula rasa* humans - and the rest of whatever and whoever co-exists here on this dark, depleting and hungry dualism extending from earth out into space, galaxies and superclusters and time as a visible film of light matter.

image: a crash site on Mars.

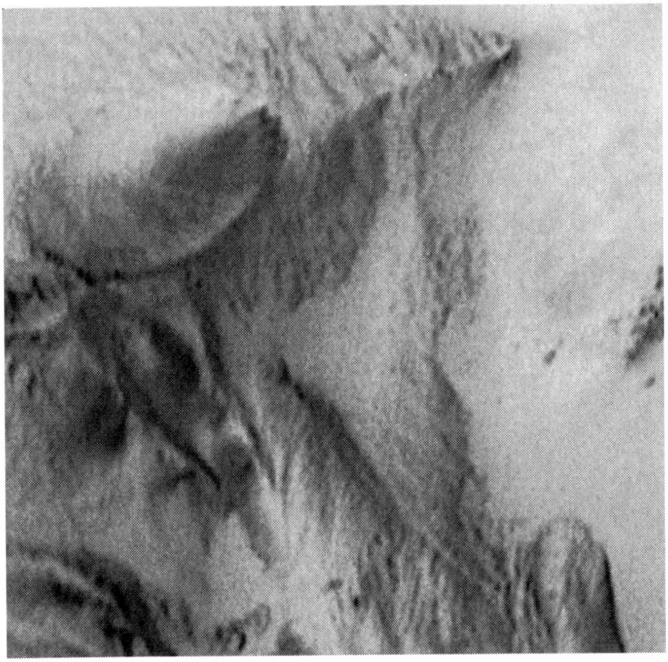

This latter stretching over the surface of an allegedly continually expanding bubble as far as our big astro-telescopes e.g. the Hubble, can see.

Somehow humanity, obsessed with its mentality and powers of reason and rather proud of its various podia and pedestals and towers of Babel has those who have been given the time to fret - temporarily removed from issues of; sustenance, water, education and health - on some long linear and totally isolated interstellar trip between the stars inside a tin can. The established hope is allegedly that they can by meeting more kinds of humanoids improve the performance of their own 'well-travelled' *hi-tek* can of beans.

Human Beings on planet earth, though, will not perform at the same level of skills and data processing and retention as the souls here with interstellar capacities and memories. Nowhere, however, is a human being proper going to discover in human culture much if any reference or evidence to the full extent of the nature of telepathic sentience amongst the general population. It is a taboo subject, even amongst the 'conspiracy authors' like Icke.

Also, nowhere is the blank slate *tabula rasa* human being going to get any information on the general and almost universal ability of sentiently processing souls to enact ultra-massive data recognition, upload and processing. This information tends to be wrapped up in a sub-culture of superhuman comics and cartoons - encouraging people/humans to climb mountains and stay in ice caves for years whilst practising insane gymnastics blindfold - all this to compete with 'Dragons'.

e.g. The fantasy action movie 'Kung Fu Hustle' where an escalation of ever more bizarre conflicts leads the hero from the mundane physical art into the paradigm of superhuman antics and magic is probably honest ..

It may be, though, that there are actually several things 'going on' at once here on Earth.

e.g.s: a gulag for captured sentient alien life utilising Human DNA and hitek soul recycling controls, or, the Race of Adam - vying with temptations and choice to test themselves to the limits of life over whether they will follow Christ or fall into bad, Godless ways, or, organic soul farmers benefitting from the harvest of soul-juices released when their other sorts of captives are artificially distressed by. e.g. contrived desolation by feats of 'godlike' prowess designed to crush emergent egos etc

image: dead alien with hand gun under slab of housing rubble, Gale Crater, Mars, courtesy NASA.

re-wiping the slate clean

Speculation could be that with e.g. Mars showing signs of being involved in an interstellar conflagration - the history of that - appears to belong to the bulldozers of the alien victors. The same 'victors' whose interdimensional behaviour and gestation, feeding and birthing processes appear at best neutral to being human on Earth.

The Martian surface appears to have had a lot going for it before its desertification.

Those interested in dynasty and continuity here on Earth, are happy to play on the swings and roundabouts of 'karma'. The latter moving between the fleeting and temporary shells with inborn and retained knowledge that resonates with attachments to other things that are passing away to greater or lesser extents. Humans can either choose to get dragged into this ongoing process and then get 'milked' like cattle, or, in connecting or reconnecting with the good things in their being, choose the highest pathway, disconnecting from the claws of death, facing towards the light of home.

I doubt that any human being can find their way out of *'Plato's Cave'* on Earth without assistance from the High Realms of Heaven.
Plato thought that human life on Earth could be characterised as the movement of shadows from participants on the back of a cave wall, The truth and light of reality shining from behind in all its fullness and glory is not yet seen.
Whereas the allegedly captured and soul-recycled starship pilots and galactic dissidents and investors tend to treat the deliberately degraded infrastructure on Earth as an amusing charade for one reason or another - they never cease to cause most

clueless humans to lose themselves and disorientate themselves in it all.

◆ ◆ ◆

JOCK TAMSON'S BAIRNS ?

image: antique steam train from the 'Age of Steam'.

Scottish for we are all the same under the skin - that we've all got the one root or source i.e. Mr Tamson etc - though today I am not certain that the old saying, *'we are a' Jock Tamson's Bairns'* is true.

With plenty of other 'wise' old Scottish sayings to choose from though such as; 'an apple doesn't fall far from the tree' equiva-

lent to - 'like father - like son' etc at some point our understanding and experience of 'dynasty and privilege' on Earth is going to diverge.
Some have it easy before the facts of life here - and some clearly do not.

So here is my shortlist of some of the possible Draconian attitudes towards HU-mans [i.e. Humans: blank slate people born with no innate advantages.]

1. Monkeys are disinterested, unfocussed and unable to process or retain information and ideas and skills in a detailed, sustained or applied way.
2. Monkeys cannot achieve excellence and are therefore liable to anger, jealousy and bitterness towards those who achieve
3. Monkeys have little interest in or affinity with the earthly cycle of life and energies and are therefore akin to un-resonant wood.
4. Monkeys cannot feel or experience things as intensely as other humanoids on Earth
5. Monkeys have little capacity for any enlightenment

on Earth

6. *Monkeys are going to Heaven anyway so send them on their way with a good spiritual, mental and physical kicking. E.G. (2 Peter 3:13 Nevertheless we, according to his promise, look for new heavens and a new earth, wherein dwelleth righteousness.)*

There have evidently been wars and conflicts in this galaxy - see the quotes below - but just what happens to the prisoners in these conflicts ?

'Q. what are the Beings doing with the other ones ? A. looking at them, touching them with something, real fast. Q. you mean, with an instrument of some sort ?. A. Yeah with a stick .. and they're all quiet.'

Jacobs DM, 'Alien Encounters - first-hand accounts of UFO abductions', pub. 1994, Virgin, ISBN 0-86369-727-5, p.76

Also from some of the Cosmic history, e.g. Orion conflicts, however biased from Alex Collier, and also in our own older accounts of Draconian/reptilian mythology, e.g. the Book of Enoch and the prisoner army called 'The Grigori', the Bible, Enki, and museum artefacts, monumental statues e.g. City of London, and the witness accounts of Draco battleships and warfare from e.g. Susan Reed, 'Jewels' and James Bartley.

Moreover, in a galaxy that has for millennia been party to the wars and tribulations of the Reptilian and other species that have been mentioned variously from e.g. abductee accounts it is clear that if there was going to be any benevolent change in the Status Quo on Earth enforced by some space fleet of liberation - that it would have happened by now in one of the many millennia since the Sphinx was first built.

Looking after their quarry

Indeed NASA recently announced [c.a. 2018] that the rings of Saturn were almost totally disintegrated. A fly-past by the Cassini probe recently imaged one of the long cylindrical ships amongst the crunched up debris in the rings that had been spotted almost 50 years previously in the 1970's by Scottish astronomer Norman Bergrun and written of in his 'Ringmakers of Saturn' a phenomenon probably better described with 21st Century hindsight as the 'Ringminers of Saturn' !

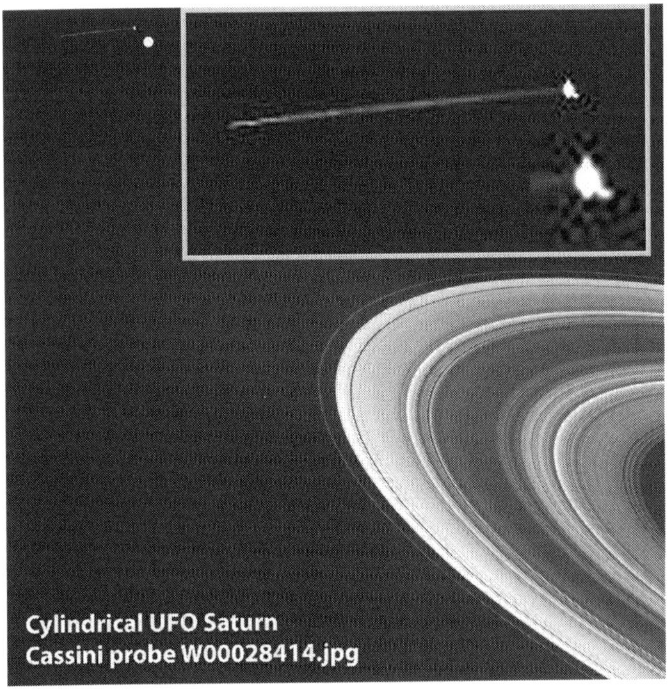

You can see from some of the ideas presented here that Earth's history and its current cultural reality as a standalone 'human' idea that starts with humanity (*homo sapien*) evolving in Africa with stones and bones and slowly moves up some scale of evolution through technology is rather farcical. [e.g. in light of the empirical finds and reports in; Cremo, M, 'Forbidden Archaeology', 2001]

There are abundant examples of interstellar conflict in our galaxy, and I have personally conversed with two people who have memories of interstellar life and conflict before they were allegedly captured and recycled here.

[e.g. Jewels and her family (soul group) alleged capture in the Pleiadian constellation from the times of Egypt,

on the run in 20th Century America from an ominous and darkly possessive island-owning Reptilian Overlord using small shuttle-ships to abduct and shuttle her to unhappy sounding places.

and; Paul Schroeder - at one point feeling dread for his life-essences in some dark, alien, harvesting process, and Ralph, a former US Intelligence Accountant in possession of memories from some war in the constellation of Orion]

Whilst our last thousand years is replete with flying shields and medieval wood-engraved UFOs that also posed over European skies to be in Renaissance paintings: so few of the sighted ET ships over the millennia were actually alleged to be doing anything to alter the deliberately artificial and primitive charade and its alien-engineered despair.

behind the scenes

All the millennia of mud and damp wood, bows and arrows, sails and stone walls were actually totally un-necessary and totally unreflective of the Interstellar powers behind the sometimes cheap and flimsy theatrical staging on this planets surface.

Why therefore in millennia of interstellar reality at least under the Earth - from those days till now, have the controlling Reptilian elite retained and engineered a debilitating disease ridden pigsty and technological cul-de-sac when even as interstellar prisoners peoples could have been processed amongst hi-tek metallic spires and walkways in more hygienic and rationally performing though albeit oppressive conditions ?

The answer lies in the existential distress and disease inflicted by deliberately obsolete and malfunctioning materials and processes that are forced upon our straight-jacketed HU-man souls for that distress, like organic lemon-juice squeezed out of bitterness, is a desired reality for the waning and soul-juice hungry Reptilian civilisation.

The Greys also here performing in a janitorial capacity have their own deliberate agenda of strip-mining the detainees .. e.g. Nigel Kerner - 'The Song of the Greys.'

Amongst this dysfunctional charade however strut the turbocharged gods of excellence and easy experts of everything you ever personally wanted or were made to think you wanted to do or achieve. Often the unjust winners and losers serve to stir the pot.

The phoney and chaotic and often surreal and evil charades serve to keep us focussed, hyper-vigilant and deliberately, spiritually suppressed.

Indeed for some, there never seems enough time to be thankful, reflect and pray or even recognise a need for inner peace,

What is a Human Being though and why is it that we are made to think by many people that there are no Reptilians currently on the planets surface [e.g. Bob Dean, Bill Deagle, Z Sitchin, etc]. Evidently, cities on the contrary, are saturated with Reptilian veneration and monumental works to them both ancient and modern. [e.g. the Vatican audience hall]

Obviously [from Masonic lore] there are a bunch of Beings called the HU ... and then there are the HU-mans, and also - perhaps as curators or farm help, shapeshifting Greys/Faeries [British Calendar Customs IM Banks, 1937 vol.1-3]

In view of the fact that there are many human people on this planet who now see a soul farm instead of some society never quite getting there whether; scientifically, technologically, medically, socially, politically or spiritually - it's time I think that we amnesiac, artificially distressed and deliberately thwarted humans stopped thinking like victims and whining like unhappy cattle.

We can see that the planets surface has been inhabited by beings with interstellar capacity for millennia, both underground and overground, and that what we take for the story of human history and evolution has been severely engineered.

e.g. a soul farming scenario akin to the matrix ideas described by Drew Hempel and Mat Delooze, Paul Schroeder, Whitley

Streiber, Alex Collier, Nigel Kerner and others.

In this alleged aeon-old evil industry of soul crimes both Reptilian and Greys [e.g. devils; naga, Anunnaki, seelie court, etc, and, demons; djinn, elementals, archons, faeries, un-seelie court, etc] in a symbiotic relationship strip out the souls of their captives and assimilate them by subjecting them to the exact negation of their; spiritual, moral, artistic, sexual/social, creative and re-creative aspirations and abilities.

We collectively over seven billion of us stay on the planet's surface and for the overwhelming majority of those Billions of people - is life in states of Bronze Age deprivation; slavery to financiers, governments, militaries and industries comparable to the slaves of Sumeria and Egypt many thousands of years BC.

When we see the facts that it's likely the slaves of ancient Egypt had better living conditions, and little toxins in their food and drink, and were less numerous - they in many ways had it better then than the majority of the worlds population in the 21st Century.
In the 'west' - some people - a tiny percentage of IT literate population - may wave their iPhones and go on about advanced medicine - but today's medicine isn't always designed to cure things, more to treat symptoms and our tablets download information that is increasingly corrupted by controlling political interests. The information contained in today's tablets is not immutably etched in time like that in the tablets Moses brought down from Mount Sinai.

e.g. it is very unlikely you will find a full and 'unabridged' digital copy of Josephus Flavius's 'History of the Jews' which includes or even references the chapter that mentions the names and purposes of some of the 'fallen angels'. e.g. Samael a dark leader.

Beyond the relative hi-tek comforts within our tiny pockets of semi-technological half-working OK stuff is the extensive reality faced by billions of others.

"If you have food in the refrigerator, clothes on your back, a roof overhead and a place to sleep you are richer than 75% of this world."

"If you have money in the bank, in your wallet, and spare change in a dish, you are wealthier than 92 % of people on Earth, and if you read this on your own device, you are part of the 1% in the world who has that opportunity."

"If you have never experienced the fear in battle, the loneliness of imprisonment, the agony of torture, or the pangs of starvation... You have more privilege than over 700 million people in the world."

"If you can attend a place of faith or worship without the fear of harassment, arrest, torture or death you are looked up to by, and more blessed than, three billion people in the world."

"If you can read this and see it on either on paper or on a device, you seem more blessed than at least two billion people in the world who cannot read at all."

To get to the world of many mansions and palaces in the heavens promised by Christ we may need to reach out beyond a whole bunch of superhuman beings that operate at every level within the infrastructure of our society.

Their main reason I think for enforcing this desolate primitivism on the planets surface whilst enjoying the comforts of the interstellar civilisations underground is for reasons that are not loving and good.

image: monumental debris, Gale Crater, Mars, NASA/JPL, Spirit Rover

It may be that Earth's surface ends up looking like Mars as the last generations of Earth are finally harvested, ending a long-lasting and well-maintained charade.

Instead of mud huts and smelly 'Knights in Shining Armour' - for millennia we, as a people, could have wanted for no comforts, been free and enabled to be a loving and socially productive interstellar and interdimensional society.

organic bitter lemons

If the Anunnaki allegedly fell here for gold [Sitchin, Z] - it wouldn't be the metallic gold they could easily fuse and fabricate from more base material atoms with their technology and abundant free (electrical) energy. Rather it would be to make desolate and feed off the spiritually golden souls of the (Human) Race of Adam.

The one sort of energy these beings cannot innately depend on having is the life-energy from their own soul, having made it scarce on choosing to disconnect from their Source.
What better way can evil try to taunt the Father they willingly disconnected from in the Fall - but by enslaving and making desolate the creative processes of this world and the ensouled peoples on it.

If Earth's status quo was just about playing recycling games with soul captives, then the planet could easily have been covered in; advanced metallic architecture, grand reptilian city designs and interstellar class social infrastructure and transportation based on free energy. Earth indeed could have been this way for 20 millennia since the alleged fall of Atlantis.
There have evidently been wars and conflicts in this galaxy - see the quotes below - but just what happens to the prisoners in these conflicts ?

The prisoners of war [e.g. the Grigori, from the 'Book of Enoch'] could have been rendered in an advanced looking interstellar environment but totally controlled by wearable controls and containment and then butchered as per usual status quo on some full moon or at whatever party without ever having to resort to the desolate social deserts and low class circuses of Earth.

The key to the alleged soul-farming-by-distress on Earth therefore is;

1. the socially engineered desolation and false visions of historic activity. This whilst driving some sort of end-based social progress towards some imaginary social goal. (donkey with

blinkers and carrot and stick incentives)

2. deliberate obsolescence and inbuilt failures in all tools, mechanisms and social processes.

3. the creation of a context-specific and targeted personal hell for the captives maintained and moderated by both Reptilian and Grey technologies and innate skills. The qualities and properties of this individual experience are intended to negate and distress and distort our best personal qualities and abilities - such that our distress can be milked by deceit and distressing and disconnection of the soul by disorientation.

4. The affectation, control and sabotage of the human captive mind via natural and technological and social abilities and processes. These may include dysfunctional human 'education' of the blank slate or tabula rasa and, the hijacking of our creative intentions. Our easily perceived intentions represent energy and spiritual investments in these things we think we want to do.

5. the physical dustification and desolation of all life by oxidation and fission, entropy and disorder, material distress and spiritual disassociation, calumny and disintegration.

The Repto-Grey [devil-demon] soul farming paradigm on Earth though is not about social justice for humans or very much about personal growth opportunities for human individuals it is, rather, about the stripping of the souls in lesser containers that are down on the farm.

The 'numero uno', alpha draconis therefore is a self-made, self-perpetuating all-star predator within a hierarchy where if *'do what thou wilt'* [Crowleigh, A (Law of Thelema)] was indeed all of the law .. then the biggest swamp monster always comes out on top.

The Reptilians may also have a secondary objective down on

the farm here .. and that is the creation of suitable biological containers as dimensional anchors in which to gestate and nurture and feed and orientate their evil ancestral swamp larvae.

It is probably beneficial to the incoming proto-Reptilians that the artificially primitive socially engineered environment is a basic and primitive analogy of the greater interstellar reality. The nature of a chaotic swamp demon might be more able to get a basic social orientation and primary education in a bounded prisoner; a lightweight version of interstellar ideologies. These creatures when inserted into blanked human beings can watch and learn from the more evolved souls as they struggle with redundancies in social tools and processes.

The tertiary product of the soul farm for the Reptilians e.g. as espoused in the first twenty minutes of the film 'The Golden Compass' where the hungry beings are encouraged by the presence of a rich seam of soul dust to enrich themselves with - to give their living death more sparkle.
In this context, endless 'new-age channels' that invite us to think of ourselves as stardust, electrons, photons have us resonate with an end product of annihilation and death.

Reptilian Naga soul-groups are mentioned in Spiritual theosophy and many of these ideologies espouse emptiness and emptying and surrender. On any other planet in the Cosmos that has had no ET soul capture matrix and telepathic technology deployed for thousands of years that is maybe a good recreational and spiritual idea.

The things we take for granted as part of our daily lives on planet Earth is that someway and somehow - some progress has been made with the invention of sciences, medicines and technologies - and that some way back there have been wars and older wars and older technologies and more primitive cultures and that somehow a banana eating ape then progressed from the African savannah in an orderly and logical way - through the coffee shops of the Italian Renaissance, travelling the world in unhappy ships for the price of a loaf of bread and who then developed all the science and technology that we all appreciate in the 21st Century today, having made a hundred thousand years of adaptation, war and natural selection.

We can see the proof of this in our media and culture, our films and our books, our children's educational material - this idea that back then wasn't as modern or as good as now.

The problem with this linear evolutionary scale and ladder as portrayed is that it is a fallacy.
There are accounts of Space Age technology in our folklore e.g. the Mahabarata and other Vedic lore. We also see the proof that highly technological extra terrestrial culture has been taking off from places in and around our towns and cities in e.g. Europe, South and Meso America, China, India, Australia and Scandinavia and the Holy land for thousands of years ... so how is it therefore that we as a people call ourselves the 'human race' but that itself is a fallacy that 'humans' or all that appears human are one kind of being descended from a dysfunctional primate.

There are *tabula rasa* - blank slated amnesiac humans - and then there are whole cultures of shape shifters e.g. Greys, Naga, Skinwalkers etc
I found it interesting that in Chinese mythology, godlike beings fly through the air and make war like the Japanese Ogre Magi.
In Celtic mythology, the Light Lance of the god Lugh sounds like a heavy phaser weapon from Star Trek.

From my own personal experience I have seen beings move beyond the time frames and sensory capacities of the real human being, and these others live amongst us.
Humans by comparison live in slow motion.
From satellite photographs you can see some of these beings streaking from the windows of their houses, or indeed a local cameraman films balls of light manifesting a return from a UFO

on Saturday night .. the neighbours perhaps having gone out for a pint of some convivial and essential fluid refreshment at the Lunar Hilton.

For the rest of us we have our distractions .. the political circus, the dangers of war and mass extinction, evil fanatics etc Vandals, Huns, Goths, Saladin, King John, Caligula, Machiavelli, Napoleon, Stalin, Hitler, 21st Century population reduction and 'sustainable globalism' - from age to age the darkness of evil howls at our door.
It is clear that even from the accounts of 17th and 18th century England and Scotland that alien abductions were proceeding for various reasons such as those given by Paul Schroeder in 21st Century USA http://www.iwasabducted.com/schroeder/tactics.htm

The human race though is drip-fed the impression that science and rational people are somehow moving us forward. Today this is more often viewed for the cynical joke that it is.

Planned obsolescence

Given centuries of secret, advanced and benign extra terrestrial neighbours therefore .. why are we not all flying about in anti-gravity chariots, why are humans not checking out our galactic stock options by now, or our new real estate on a new terra-forming project. Why are we not using the free energy that was available to Faraday at the end of the 19th century or Tesla and Townsend Brown at the beginning of the 20th Century?
The old excuses of vested interests in the Petrodollar actually don't wash .. because in truth our extra terrestrial brothers and sisters who may have been holding humanity in this dumbed down funny farm and stagnant cul-de-sac could have introduced anti-gravity long before the invention of the internal combustion engine and the petroleum paradigm.

Neither does the excuse that 'we' don't deserve it - who is 'we' anyway ?
What is 'we' is more the truth in my opinion.

More than just 'we the (Adamic) human race'.

In any case, even in terms of our human Disneyland, Oil companies could simply have bought the antigravity monopoly to preserve the stock market status quo.

(Much like the emerging railway companies were bought by the Canal entrepreneurs to maintain the monopoly on infrastructure in the 19th Century Industrial Revolution in England.)
Basically there ought to have been nothing wrong with us having interstellar chariots in Egyptian or Sumerian times.
e.g. the Vimana - flying ships in the Mahabarata

In fact the only thing *'unsustainable'* on this planet is not the massive resource-hungry and growing population [UN Agenda 21] – but the bunch of more and more obvious lies that keep it and us shackled to its primitivism.

Some might say that 'we' did, x,y,z to the Earth, or rather the Anunnaki Reptilian overlords did.
Why were the flying shields reported overflying Greece and Rome not merely part of a larger interstellar sociological infrastructure under more overt *hi-tek* control.
So why are we not even as slaves flying about/conveyed in antigravity sleds between impressive interstellar metallic domes and spires.
Why then the millennia of plagues, wars, starvation and ignorance in a basic, unsupplied, unsanitary conditions.
Why were the grand designs of the Renaissance not enacted in a sumptuous interstellar canvas of high technology and art-form and more technologically produced Reptilian slavery ...

Basically why are we all staggering about between cardboard boxes, mud huts and all the dysfunctional planned obsolescence and entropy, instead of as mere slaves with some sort of *hi-tek* collar and computer monitoring making the coffee, doing the housework and going missing on the night of some full moon etc but at least being driven to some unhappy dark altar in some sort of *hi-tek* conveyance without the use of an internal combustion engine.

We can argue that we are being farmed and processed as physical slaves but that argument isn't sufficient to explain a planet of historical contradictions and strangely behaving zones and spiritual nihilism.

If you look at all the historical infrastructure that alleges to be human in the last 20,000 years on Earth - none of it had to be that way at all.
It could all have been gleaming spires and domes and anti-gravity sleds and energy to matter and matter-to-matter manufacturing etc.
None of the social order we take as being human was necessary at all - for we can surmise that non-humans with interstellar knowledge and ability have been running the planets surface and its more ancient underground since at least the Wars of the Fall of Atlantis.

On a farm where the farmers at a moments notice can step forward and outshine the efforts of the more basic genetic herd at almost any task, trade, art or artifice without much prior experience or training it does rather seem that the main players and sideshow owners in this brutal charade appear to have god-like aptitudes to do everything except make the place harmless.

The basic genetic herd perhaps capped and dumbed down and less resonant and tuned in, to lightning-like processes and powers of reason and uptake, are likely to be compared to wood.

If the basic wooden-minded human herd are being in some way

milked amongst all the harm it would suggest that even though the irises of their eyes remain static and do not open into long reptilian slits or have eyes that can turn jet black, or, are somehow networked into a data and skill-sharing process - disconnected human beings - however wooden in demeanour do have something to offer our hungry un-human demi-gods. We have been 'encouraged' to supply them with high quality organic soul-distress - biomagnetic distress for millennia.

Certainly if suddenly a space-age hi-tek Utopia would suddenly manifest on the planets surface instead of a distress farm with a theme of desolation and burning things - all human distress would be over.

Indeed the classical vision of hell and purgatory appears to enact itself out in the burning of - fission of; trees, natural processes, atoms, of malignant beings creating ashes and dust most of it toxic.

For the disconnected human being though the ultimate racism is that they have a feeling of not being part of the revellers and staff on the farm and that the people who are, seem to enjoy riding about in horses and carts equipped with advanced sound systems whilst simultaneously multitasking with hi-tek laptops developing and planning a series of gizmos with a short life cycle which will quickly be obsolete and part of the litter on the planetary rubbish tip.

Humans not plugged into the song of desolation mindset tend to seek Heaven and probably thanks to the many Angels and Saints that come here to minister to their souls many find the stairway out.

In the meantime though the next time we see youtubes of some 9 year old playing high-speed jazz sonatas in a recording studio with other older professional musicians and despite having no way to hear what they are doing execute the most incredible harmonies and part playing we have to come to the conclusion that there are things happening which are outrageously unfair to human nature.

Although human-baiting [cf. cultural appropriation] may seem amusing at the time to the Anunnaki overlords and their demonic janitors - the future outlook for the advancement of human souls in heavens above looks better aspected than that of the reptilians fallen down here. The latter appear to be currently struggling in a Tolkeinesque way with the demonic matrix of the Greys which looks set to ultimately consume them like a hungry nihilistic ring of power.

There again the overlords were always feeling precious ...

So when we humans get born into 'Jurassic Park' and we turn up as a genetically un-resonant non-telepath we are usually born [with a 'hard brain' cf. the Secret School of Theosophy] in the west into fully or partially functional telepathic families whose reptilian brains and ancestral functionality are operational to a greater or lesser extent. We the un-resonant relative deadwood are instantly buffered by our choices and genetics from the jungle screams and feeding frenzy of raging predatory Dinosaurs.

Be they social or anti-social predators the vibrant rage of Draco going physically or spiritually head-to-head is almost totally silenced in the awakened human baby.

It might be that we didn't communicate with signals in or out of the womb or were not responding to or joining in to the jungle chorus - but at some point I believe that we are directly approached in a mind-to-mind/spirit communication and given a choice.

Are you for being IN the Draco hivesong or OUT the Draco hivesong ?

If in - then as Tony Blair once said - things can only get better.

For many non-human beings on planet Earth who can move distances between the blink of a human eye, or who can teleport themselves and far/remote view or shapeshift themselves and their appearance, and fashionably remodify themselves at a whim .. life on planet Earth can be somewhat of a breeze.

Of course those with overlordish powers seem to accrue all the social advantages by use and misuse of telepathy.
If we look closer though we can see that for society and its alleged advantages; the gold plating has lost its shine, the fruit its flavour, the moth taken the emperors clothes and dust clings to the dark and dubious transactions of numerous social charades in an engaging but fruitless impersonation of a real society.

Many human beings, themselves genetically incapacitated, slower to process, more biology than spirit always seem to be on some fatal and oppressive treadmill from which they are discouraged and dissuaded from leaving.
The cycle of the wheel of time.

Dr HU

The Druids had a high veneration for the Serpent. Their great god, Hu, was typified by that reptile; and he is represented by the Bards as *'the wonderful chief Dragon, the sovereign of heaven'.*" George Oliver, Signs and Symbols, New York, Macoy Publishing and Masonic Supply Company, 1906, p. 36

"Masons .. admire the Druids and some of them even claim that Masonry came from Druidism. Of course, the Druids were occultic priests, practiced astrology, and offered human sacrifices." Dr. C. Burns, Masonic and Occult Symbols Illustrated, p. 28.

Dr Deagle and Eastern teaching and Masonic teaching define the HU of 'human' to be the Reptilian and god source and the man of the HUman to be the clay or nesting material in which the ancestral spawn of the Reptilians are to be parasitically gestated and groomed by our own personal stresses and strains amongst the dysfunctional social mess and its worldly evils.
A HUman therefore is a being of part Reptilian DNA and part animalistic clay or nesting material empowered by a captive soul into which the Reptilian administrators or farmers attempt to insert their ancestral seedstock to be nannied.
The occult "Royal Human" [i.e. host] therefore is a ripe and fruitful 'repto nest', [host] and also an active teacher in anthropomorphic problem solving strategies. Other issues that may be taught in the habitation of such Earth-bound human forms; e.g. actively striving to keep balance and order and nurture and walk the middle line amongst the artificial chaos.

At the right time the Reptilian and Grey farmers crack open a bunch of gestating nests or Humans in some brutal harvesting process e.g. a war and from the ashes and broken down soul embers of this trauma - emerges the Phoenix or Hrumachis the fully educated Reptilian adolescent child [Horus] that has learned all the lessons needed from the artificially induced strife in the life of its HU-man host.

There is, however, lots of evidence for highly good sentient Angelic beings at work amongst the darkness here, and in my own life too. Without that connection there is little hope.

It can be seen from the following biblical quotes, one used by three of the world's major religions that there was anciently a paradigm of translation and remaking by the will of the Holy Spirit and that this process of translation applied itself to social and ideological changes and also to the remaking and rescripting of peoples Biology and mortality.

NOT LOST IN THE TRANSLATION

image: the author in contemplation on St Margaret's Stone, Dunfermline.

There is hope therefore that despite being on a planet full of dragons and their 'pleasant palaces' Isaiah 13:22 - that a greater down-pouring of life and energy and will from higher spheres and frequencies will infuse our world and its peoples.

2 Samuel 3:10 To translate the kingdom from the house of Saul, and to set up the throne of David over Israel and over Judah, from Dan even to Beersheba

Colossians 1:13 Who hath delivered us from the power of darkness, and hath translated us into the kingdom of his dear Son:

Attachment to the world and the things in it is a decaying disease illustrated in many Eastern beliefs and their religions. It can pull our vision into a cycle of death. There are Reptilian Naga soul groups factored into and facilitated by an eastern Religion that centres on detachment from the world e.g. Buddhism.

1 John 2:15 Love not the world, neither the things that are in the world. If any man love the world, the love of the Father is not in him.
16 For all that is in the world, the lust of the flesh, and the lust of the eyes, and the pride of life, is not of the Father, but is of the world.
17 And the world passeth away, and the lust thereof: but he that doeth the will of God abideth for ever.

The hope however for us all in these end days may not arrive in a flying saucer or by the emissaries of a false prophet with alleged signs and wonders or hopeless promise. Our own ticket up and away is not necessarily a ticket to anywhere in this galaxy in some ship transported by non-humans who have aided and abetted the aberrant status quo on this world.
In the New Testament, and also in other works on this planet

there is evidence of a high energy over matter way of being. When applied to mankind - humanity - however, 'Men' can become 'Xmen'.

Hebrews 11:5 By faith Enoch was translated that he should not see death; and was not found, because God had translated him: for before his translation he had this testimony, that he pleased God.

John 21:21 Peter seeing him saith to Jesus, Lord, and what shall this man do?
22 Jesus saith unto him, If I will that he tarry till I come, what is that to thee? follow thou me.
23 Then went this saying abroad among the brethren, that that disciple should not die: yet Jesus said not unto him, He shall not die; but, If I will that he tarry till I come, what is that to thee?

Practitioners in possession of these miraculous abilities can without the aid of a cloning pod or a vat of green jelly or some strange juices revivify and spiritually remake people who would have passed on.

Acts 20:9 And there sat in a window a certain young man named Eutychus, being fallen into a deep sleep: and as Paul was long preaching, he sunk down with sleep, and fell down from the third loft, and was taken up dead.
10 And Paul went down, and fell on him, and embracing him said, Trouble not yourselves; for his life is in him.
11 When he therefore was come up again, and had broken bread, and eaten, and talked a long while, even till break of day, so he departed.
12 And they brought the young man alive, and were not a little comforted.

Acts of intervention by the Holy Spirit have been recorded throughout history when the bonds between ourselves and these worldly densities can be loosened. On the more sinister side - we know that some alien species are more than able to float abductees through walls – so how much more can be done with love etc

Acts 12:6 And when Herod would have brought him forth, the same night Peter was sleeping between two soldiers, bound with two chains: and the keepers before the door kept the prison.
7 And, behold, the angel of the Lord came upon him, and a light shined in the prison: and he smote Peter on the side, and raised him up, saying, Arise up quickly. And his chains fell off from his hands.
8 And the angel said unto him, Gird thyself, and bind on thy sandals. And so he did. And he saith unto him, Cast thy garment about thee, and follow me.
9 And he went out, and followed him; and wist not that it was true which was done by the angel; but thought he saw a vision.
10 When they were past the first and the second ward, they came unto the iron gate that leadeth unto the city; which opened to them of his own accord: and they went out, and passed on through one street; and forthwith the angel departed from him.
11 And when Peter was come to himself, he said, Now I know of a surety, that the Lord hath sent his angel, and hath delivered me out of the hand of Herod, and from all the expectation of the people of the Jews.

It could be at some point though that bouts of miraculous heavenly healing and relocation will take place amongst peoples on Earth in the 21st century with or without the intercession of some dubious earth-bound flunkies in a space ship.

◆◆◆

WHAT IS TRUE ?

There has always been a very ancient idea running through global folklore in all millennia and cultures that there are sub-surface cities within a hollow earth, and that at the heart of the hollow earth is a sun-like plasma ball radiating light and life to vegetation and creatures alike.

And we hear stories that under the Mediterranean 'holiday' islands of Majorca are cavern systems belonging to a non-human (allegedly reptilian) species.

To get that theory in perspective however, it would mean that Agencies such as NASA were economical with the truth when it came to pictures of polar entrances from their satellites etc

In a world of easy to manipulate and process digital media for example, it can never be solely shown by any digital image what is true or false.

Perhaps some evidential digital photo plus other corroborating evidence from its context would be better ?
Or perhaps it's better to rely on witness testimony from before the digital age - if, that is - it too hadn't been edited on the net before we found it.

I know that there is a net archive with Josephus Flavius's History of the Jews that would have been useful if it had retained the chapters that you can still find in the original 19th Century reference book, a very large bound, hard copy on the fallen angels and their modus operandi.

Useful also because it would have been able to back-up my assertion that the fallen giants and their progeny also mentioned in the Celtic 'Book of Invasions' - had agreed to abide underground, millennia ago.

e.g. the illustrative painting by John Duncan, 1912, called 'the Riders of the Sidhe' - The 'Sidhe' pronounced 'shee' were the noble high elves or [reptilian/aquatic] Draco alluded to in many faerie story collections from Scotland.

obfuscation

Nor must we make the other mistake of assuming that just because it is on the net, looks good etc that it is necessarily true.

Indeed there are many sites on the net employing writers and digital artists to manufacture fake news.

e.g. Image: the 'global and Hindu' swastika on the horse harness was creatively replaced on some internet archives - switching gender and not now representing the story the artist originally intended. An uneducated and probably inappropriate attempt to de-Nazify the negative associations of the swastika because of the misuse of this ancient Hindu (Male) symbol for the Sun. Some well-meaning 'policing' of 'correct thought' and its policies by artist or artists unknown change the male swastika on the horse harness - back right - to the female gnostic symbol for the female part called the 'vescica pisces'. It might be in 'context' but that doesn't make the change and deception right.

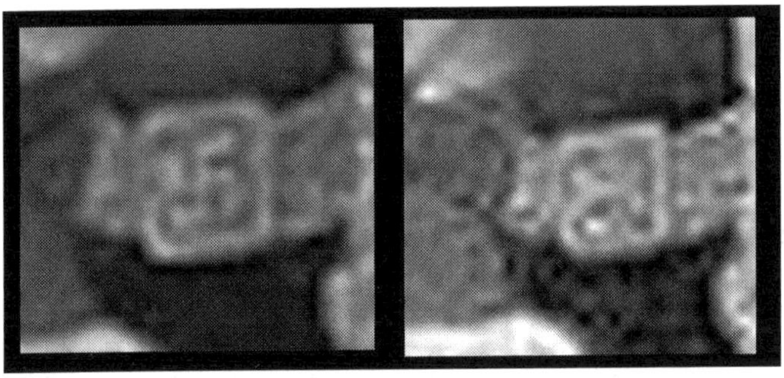

We must neither, be naïve about the status of some controversial information - for example if the net is purposefully flooded with fake images of e.g. Martian architecture and beings or Gigantic Americans - we must avoid being pushed to the conclusion that, given the deliberate nonsense, there is smoke without fire. The reverse is true - there is no smoke without fire !

Some folklore speaks of hi-tek ideas such as ships or flying chariots that can unleash the power of the sun e.g. in the Mahabarata or. of beautiful cities with elevators and colourful shimmering walls, or with the capacity to project fields and beams with which to control the technologies of the surface dwellers. (Admiral Byrd's 'secret diary')

I am certain that today though, in the 21st Century, the human tunnelling machines that gave us Area 1 to Area 51 to Area 151 etc and underground corporate-sponsored mega-cities linked by high speed monorails [Schneider, P] and a certain amount of elite military paranoia have probably already been invited to forget all about going any deeper !!

The sub-surface of our planet has to be a very interesting socio-logical ecosystem and pseudo-political infrastructure full of humanoid species of all shapes and sizes and states of peace.

A 'United Sub-Surface Nations' might be an interesting place to hang out.

Stories of highly advanced military weaponry do infer or imply a highly advanced technological society. For example the human military industrial complex was thought to be driven by perceptions of war and threat for it to then achieve great military and consequentially, social advances. Hence similar rationale may model non-human technological evolution etc.

The military funding of human science has had a powerful transformative effect on the practice and products of scientific research since the early 20th century. Particularly since World War I, advanced science-based technologies have been viewed as essential elements of a successful military.

In the years immediately following World War II, the military was by far the most significant patron of university science research in the U.S., and the national labs also continued to flourish. E.g. The complex histories of computer science and computer engineering were shaped, in the first decades of digital computing, almost entirely by military funding.

The need to keep up with corporate technology research

(which was receiving the lion's share of defence contracts) also prompted many science labs to establish close relationships with industry.

Given we can assume that the interior civilisation of our planet is both highly advanced and very self-sufficient and exposed to millennia of unending comforts and careful thinking etc - can we assume we have been left to shuffle about in a radio-active desert not of our own making because some naga-esque elite corporation made a decision to build several flimsy nuclear fission power plants on the coast in a notorious earthquake and tsunami zone in the Pacific ocean ?

Such a diverse and possibly motley crew from e.g. Celtic mythology was envisioned by Scottish painter John Duncan in 1912 - with his painting of the Fomorians.

https://fi.m.wikipedia.org/wiki/Tiedosto:The_Fomorians,_Duncan_1912.jpg

Duncan, from Dundee was part of the early 20th Century Celtic Revival Movement, painting themes from ethnic Celtic mythology.

LAND OF THE AMERICAN GIANTS

This concept of giants - whether of the Nephilim - the giant descendants of the fallen angels or of the giants themselves - is born out by some of the folklore.

Indeed in the USA there is a constant 'conspiracy dialogue' about the Smithsonian Institute *(pictured above)* 'covering up' the archaeological remains of a giant people. Some of it based on a very ancient Imperial Chinese survey of North America.

In the Ninth and Fourteenth Books of the Shan Hai King are fragments of observations made by the Oriental survey team of the various people inhabiting America at that time. In the regions of the "Southeast Corner to the Northeast Corner" (from Georgia to New England),as well as in the "Great Waste" (the western and south-western deserts), the Chinese called the "Great Men's Country." One of the surveyors, named Cheu-fu~Chang, found in the west not far from the "Great Canyon Where the Sun is Born"--the Grand Canyon--a wooden arrow with a metal point" 6 1/2 feet long. He calculated that its owner must have been 12 to 15 feet tall. A footnote to this discovery, given in the Fourteenth Book, tells how ancient Japanese sailors once encountered bad weather, and were driven onto the shores of the "Eastern Continent." There, before their return home, they encountered "tall savages of a foreign tribe" more than 11 feet high. Other early Chinese literature, such as Ho-tu's "Album of Gems" and the "Kuh-liang History" speak of strange lands beyond the Pacific called Ta-tsin" and "Lin-t'ao," where men of huge stature lived, leaving behind footprints many feet in size where they walked.

The alleged giants of North America appear at one time to have been a restless, warlike breed, for several ancient sources describe their invasions of other lands.

In LOST MINES AND HIDDEN TREASURE, the author Leland Lovelace tells of two prospectors who discovered a series of caves in the mountains of south-western Nevada. Within the giant caverns they discovered furniture pieces of enormous size as if they had been constructed for giants. Dishes of gold and other precious metals also were found in the caves.

It has been seen in many of the ancient mounds found in Ohio, Indiana, Pennsylvania, New York and Minnesota that giant skeletons and artefacts were unearthed. The weight of evidence therefore points to the Indians' legends possessing the historical fact--not the conservative theories.

According to the Indian (native American) accounts (as preserved in Volume 12 of 'Memoires of the Historical Society of Pennsylvania' , in the distant past the Deleware-Lenni-lenape peoples swept in a flood of migration from the far west, but on reaching the valleys west of the Mississippi, they were confronted by a well-entrenched people of tremendous stature and possessing a high civilization. These people they called the "Allegewi" or "Telligewi"--much the same as given to them by the California Indians, and after whom the Alleghany river and mountains were named.

The progress of the Deleware-Lenni-lenape was stopped, and they were driven back but not discouraged. At the same time, the Iroquois people were trying to find a passage through Allegewi territory, from the north.

Two migratory peoples eventually entered into an alliance together, and proclaimed war against the giants. One by one, the Allegewi strongholds fell, and the giants were forced to become wanderers along the streams and river-systems they had attempted to defend.

Another tradition affirms that the primitive Indian invaders, because of their great numbers, successfully overwhelmed the ancient gargantuan inhabitants of the north-central states, and that the last great battle in this area was fought at the falls of the Ohio river, where the remnant was driven upon a small island below the rapids, and there the whole of them cut to pieces.

Thc Indian chief, Tobacco, informed General George Rogers Clark of a legend in which was preserved the memory of a battle fought at Sandy Island, where "the first peoples of this land" had been slaughtered. Another Indian chief, Cornplanter, told that Ohio, Kentucky and Tennessee had once been inhabited by a gigantic white-skinned people, who were familiar with the arts of civilization, which his own forefathers knew nothing of. After a series of battles with the invading tribes, these former inhabitants were completely exterminated.

The chief also declared that the old burial places--the mounds--were the graves of these indigenous giants, and that the great earthen fortresses had not been constructed by his people, but belonged to the "very long ago" people, who were huge, light-complexioned, and skilled in many arts.

The Indians also had a superstition concerning the territory of what is now Kentucky. One Indian elder expressed his astonishment that present-day white folk would want to live in a region which had been the scene of such conflicts as had taken place there. An old Sac Indian, in 1800, said that Kentucky was filled with ghosts of its slaughtered giant inhabitants, and wondered why the white man could make it his home.

When we look at the Mound Builder earthworks in the northern and central states, it is interesting to note that they are mostly defense enclosures which, for the most part, face the north and west--the directions the Indians claim their forefathers invaded from.....

◆ ◆ ◆

NICHOLAS ROERICH

Although e.g. Nicholas Roerich may have seen a 'Vimana' or UFO in Tibet in the early 20th century - the technological and social 'apartheid' the surface dwellers on this earth have experienced for thousands of years has no sign of letting up.

Roerich's 1929 book Altai-Himalaya described a type of silvery flying disc.

Here are Roerich's words describing an event of August 5, 1927 in the Qinghai province of China, on the northeastern border of Tibet:

'On August fifth-something remarkable! We were in our camp in the Kukunor district not far from the Humboldt Chain. In the morning about half-past nine some of our caravaneers noticed a remarkably big black eagle flying above us. Seven of us began to watch this unusual bird. At this same moment another of our caravaneers remarked, "There is something far above the bird." And he shouted in his astonishment. We all saw, in a direction from north to south, something big and shiny reflecting the sun, like a huge oval moving at great speed. Crossing our camp this thing changed in its direction from south to southwest. And we saw how it disappeared in the intense blue sky. We even had time to take our field glasses and saw quite distinctly an oval form with shiny surface, one side of which was brilliant from the sun.'

Nicholas Roerich's book called " Shambala," which was published in 1930 reflected his travels in Tibet and related the Tibetan's rich hollow Earth folklore - mentioning the cities of Shambala, Shangri La, and the kingdom of Agharta.

Even in the UK, tabloids of May 1st, 2019, p13, the Yeti or 'Abominable Snowman' as recorded by the Indian army near a base camp at 17000 feet at Makalu on the Nepal/Tibet border, still inspires both fear and awe with a trail of its massive 32 inch footprints in the mountain snow.

◆ ◆ ◆

ANCIENT INDIA AND ASIA, ITS EVIDENCE

Indian folklore and ancient tracts are replete with references to an underground, very advanced and well-equipped civilisation many millennia BC.

Folklore from Ancient times in India mentions a hollow earth and its cities ..

The Puranas make several comments about the hollow Earth. One such Puranic commentary involves the Kalki avatar - that at the end of Kali Yuga, (the dark, iron Age c.a. 2025AD) the Kalki Avatar will be born in the best of Brahmin families of the city of Shambala to annihilate wrongdoers on the surface of the globe by purging them with fire. Afterwards, the general Puranic version goes that men will come from the interior of the planet to the surface to re-colonise and re-start Vedic culture. Note that Shambala is mentioned in the Puranas as a city of the planet's interior. Not only in the Puranas, but in the Tibetan collective memory also, Shambala is deemed to be a city in the Earth's interior.

In Shree Ramayana there are two scenes which are suggestive of the existence of inner areas of the Earth. After Shrimati Sitadevi had been kidnapped by Ravana, Shree Laksman swore to Rama that he would pursue the rascal even if Lakshman had to chase him to the "dark hollows of the Earth."

In chapter 8 of Kishkindya, Rama proves his ability to Sugriva by discharging an arrow which ...

"pierced through seven palms, a rock, and the innermost region of the Earth and in a minute again came back to the quiver."

Supernatural weapons also appear in Hindu mythology, and are known generally as astras. These supernatural weapons are wielded by the characters of the various Hindu texts, including those from the famous epic, the Mahabharata

Here then is a small selection of things that we can at present freely find on the net if we dig into various archives.

I'm not saying that this info in its entirety is going to be there for ever either !

For example even the Wayback Machine internet 'archive' starts losing important details with time - whilst alleging to be 'preserving knowledge' for the future of mankind -

Maybe it was just me - but try finding this !! ???

In WW II, learn how inhabitants of Nagaland came to the world's attention.

http://web.petabox.bibalex.org/web/20030104230337/http:/ www.burmastar.org.uk/nagaqueen.htm

Indian folklore and ancient tracts are replete with references to an underground and very advanced civilisation many millennia BC.

There are authentic and evidential-sounding verses from the Indian Epics about how these ancient beings flew about and made war with such nuclear weapons:

J. Robert Oppenheimer the American theoretic Physicist and

'father of the modern atom bomb has a very famous quote '"We knew the world would not be the same. A few people laughed, a few people cried. Most people were silent. I remembered the line from the Hindu scripture, the Bhagavad-Gita; Vishnu is trying to persuade the Prince that he should do his duty, and to impress him, takes on his multi-armed form and says, *'Now I am become Death, the destroyer of worlds.'* I suppose we all thought that, one way or another."

From ancient texts there is more evidence of a very advanced technological society - if only from its stories of military prowess.

In the Mahabharata, various astras are used by the warriors during their epic battles. One of them, for example, is the Sudharshana Chakra. This was the astra used by Krishna, the 8th avatar of the god Vishnu, and a major character in the Mahabharata. The Sudharshana Chakra is described as a spinning disc with 108 serrated edges. This weapon was made by Vishwakarma, the architect of the gods, from the dust of the Sun and the scraps from the Shiva's trident, and given to Vishnu by Shiva. This weapon would return to its owner after disposing of an enemy.

image: Vishnu as a 'fish'

Another astra found in the Mahabharata is the Pashupatastra. This weapon is regarded to be incredibly destructive, and capable of destroying all creation.

Yet another well-known astra in the Mahabharata is the Brahmashira, a weapon created by Brahma.

As for the Brahmashira, it has been mentioned that an area struck by this weapon would be completely destroyed, the land would be barren for twelve years, rain would not fall for the same amount of time, and everything there will become toxic. In the Mahabharata, Arjuna and Ashwatthama used the Brahmashira against each other. Fearing that the power of these two astras would destroy the world, the sages beseeched the two warriors to take back their weapons.

◆ ◆ ◆

THE NAGA

Stories of advanced shapeshifting reptilians are in stories, myth and culture all over the world. In Scottish faerie tales the 'blue men of the minches' [R Kirk] or the (water dwelling) 'Draco'.

picture - Reptilian beings/Draco - 'The riders of the Sidhe, 1912, by John Duncan, Scotland.

In India they are commonly called Naga.

The word Naga comes from the Sanskrit, and nag is the word for snake, especially the cobra, in most of the languages of India.

In Tibetan Buddhism

"Nagas [kLu] are a class of beings (often snake-like in form) that dwell in a variety of locations ranging from waterways and underground locations and also in unseen realms. These beings have their own perceptions and vary in their enlightened level as do humans and other beings.

Many Kashmiri festivals relate to Naga worship, "for example during the first snowfall, Nila, the Lord of Nagas, is worshipped. The Nagas are also propitiated in April and are related to Ira-manjari Puja and to Varuna Panchmi, which is organised in July-August."

And "in the darker half of the month of Jyeshtha, when a big festival is organised to propitiate the king Taksakyatra. The Nilamatapurana listed 527 Nagas that were worshipped in Kashmir. In the account of Abul Fazal, the court historian of Akbar, there are references to seven hundred places sacred to serpents."

The purana also points to the association of the cult of Nagas with that of Shiva. In the Mahabharata and Harivamsa texts, Shesha was considered the son of Shiva. A lesser relation was developed with regard to Vishnu as in his sheshashayi form which links the primal waters with the sleeping Vishnu.

The 'golden cities of Nagaland' are described in folklore here ..

Nilamata Purana, the ancient history of Kashmir, is centered around the original inhabitants of Kashmir, the Nagas. In the verses 232-233 it mentions their capital: "O Naga, the dwelling of the Nagas is the city named Bhogavati. Having become a Yogi that Naga-chief (Vasuki) dwells there as well as here. But with his primary body, Vasuki, protecting the Nagas, shall live in Bhogavati. O sinless one, you (also) dwell here constantly." Bhogavati is also mentioned in the Bhagavata Purana 1.11.11. Its another name is Putkari.

Bhagavata Purana gives the following description of Bila-svarga, the subterranean regions compared for their opulence to heaven (5.24.7-15):

"My dear King, beneath this earth are seven other planets, known as Atala, Vitala, Sutala, Talatala, Mahatala, Rasatala and Patala. I have already explained the situation of the planetary systems of earth. The width and length of the seven lower planetary systems are calculated to be exactly the same as those of earth.

"In these seven planetary systems, which are also known as the subterranean heavens [bila-svarga], there are very beautiful houses, gardens and places of sense enjoyment, which are even more opulent than those in the higher planets because the demons have a very high standard of sensual pleasure, wealth and influence. Most of the residents of these planets, who are known as Daityas, Danavas and Nagas, live as householders. Their wives, children, friends and society are all fully engaged in illusory, material happiness. The sense enjoyment of the demigods is sometimes disturbed, but the residents of these planets enjoy life without disturbances. Thus they are understood to be very attached to illusory happiness.

"My dear King, in the imitation heavens known as bila-svarga there is a great demon named Maya Danava, who is an expert artist and architect. He has constructed many brilliantly decorated cities. There are many wonderful houses, walls, gates, assembly houses, temples, yards and temple compounds, as well as many hotels serving as residential quarters for foreigners. The houses for the leaders of these planets are constructed with the most valuable jewels, and they are always crowded with living entities known as Nagas and Asuras, as well as many pigeons, parrots and similar birds. All in all, these imitation heavenly cities are most beautifully situated and attractively decorated.

"The parks and gardens in the artificial heavens surpass in beauty those of the upper heavenly planets. The trees in those gardens, embraced by creepers, bend with a heavy burden of twigs with fruits and flowers, and therefore they appear extraordinarily beautiful. That beauty could attract anyone and make his mind fully blossom in the pleasure of sense gratification. There are many lakes and reservoirs with clear, transparent water, agitated by jumping fish and decorated with many flowers such as lilies, kuvalayas, kahlaras and blue and red lotuses. Pairs of cakravakas and many other water birds nest in the lakes and always enjoy in a happy mood, making sweet, pleasing vibrations that are very satisfying and conducive to enjoyment of the senses.

Stories of highly advanced non-human military weaponry do infer or imply a highly advanced technological society. For example the human military industrial complex was driven by perceptions of war and threat and was generally thought to achieve great military and consequentially, social advances.

The military funding of science has had a powerful transformative effect on the practice and products of scientific research since the early 20th century. Particularly since World War I, advanced science-based technologies have been viewed as essential elements of a successful military.

In the years immediately following World War II, the military was by far the most significant patron of university science research in the U.S., and the national labs also continued to flourish. E.g. The complex histories of computer science and computer engineering were shaped, in the first decades of digital computing, almost entirely by military funding.

The need to keep up with corporate technology research (which was receiving the lion's share of defence contracts) also prompted many science labs to establish close relationships with industry.

Given we can assume that the interior civilisation of our planet is both highly advanced and very self-sufficient and exposed to millennia of unending comforts - can we assume we have been left to shuffle about in a radio-active desert not of our own making because some naga-esque elite corporation made a decision to build several flimsy nuclear fission power plants on the coast in a notorious earthquake and tsunami zone in the Pacific ocean ?

been there before ?

There are authentic and evidential-sounding verses from the Indian Epics about how these ancient beings flew about and made war with such nuclear weapons and which narrated the now familiar toxic effects of such hideous warfare:

"Gurkha, flying a swift and powerful vimana (fast aircraft) hurled a single projectile (rocket) charged with the power of the Universe (nuclear device). An incandescent column of smoke and flame, as bright as ten thousand suns, rose with all its splendour.

It was an unknown weapon, an iron thunderbolt, a gigantic messenger of death, which reduced to ashes the entire race of the Vrishnis and the Andhakas.

The corpses were so burned as to be unrecognisable.

Hair and nails fell out; Pottery broke without apparent cause, and the birds turned white.

...After a few hours all foodstuffs were infected....to escape from this fire the soldiers threw themselves in streams to wash themselves and their equipment." - The Mahabharata

"It was a weapon) so powerful that it could destroy the earth in an instant. A great soaring sound in smoke and flames - And on its sits death..." - The Ramayana.

"Dense arrows of flame, like a great shower, issued forth upon creation, encompassing the enemy... A thick gloom swiftly settled upon the Pandava hosts.

Image: A-Bomb, Nagasaki, 1945 by Charles Levy - U.S. National Archives and Records Administration, Public Domain, https://commons.wikimedia.org/w/index.php?curid=56719

All points of the compass were lost in darkness. Fierce wind began to blow upward, showering dust and gravel. Birds croaked madly... the very elements seemed disturbed. The earth shook, scorched by the terrible violent heat of this weapon. Elephants burst into flame and ran to and fro in a frenzy... over a vast area, other animals crumpled to the ground and died.
From all points of the compass the arrows of flame rained continuously and fiercely." - The Mahabharata

"It was an unknown weapon, an iron thunderbolt, a gigantic messenger of death, which reduced to ashes the entire race of the Vrishnis and the Andhakas." is to be found in Section

1 of Mausala Parva.(http://www.sacred-texts.com/hin/m16/m16001.htm).

Some folklore speaks of hi-tek ideas such as ships or flying chariots that can unleash the power of the sun e.g. in the Mahabarata or of beautiful cities with elevators and colourful shimmering walls, or with the capacity to project fields and beams with which to control the technologies of the surface dwellers. (Admiral Byrd's 'secret diary')

"It was an unknown weapon, an iron thunderbolt, a gigantic messenger of death, which reduced to ashes the entire race of the Vrishnis and the Andhakas." is to be found in Section 1 of Mausala Parva.(http://www.sacred-texts.com/hin/m16/m16001.htm).

From ancient texts there is more evidence of a very advanced technological society - if only from its stories of military prowess.

In the Mahabharata, various astras are used by the warriors during their epic battles. One of them, for example, is the Sudharshana Chakra. This was the astra used by Krishna, the 8 th avatar of the god Vishnu, and a major character in the Mahabharata. The Sudharshana Chakra is described as a spinning disc with 108 serrated edges. This weapon was made by Vishwakarma, the architect of the gods, from the dust of the Sun and the scraps from the Shiva's trident, and given to Vishnu by Shiva. This weapon would return to its owner after disposing of an enemy.

Another astra found in the Mahabharata is the Pashupatastra. This weapon is regarded to be incredibly destructive, and capable of destroying all creation.

Yet another well-known astra in the Mahabharata is the Brahmashira, a weapon created by Brahma.

As for the Brahmashira, it has been mentioned that an area struck by this weapon would be completely destroyed, the land would be barren for twelve years, rain would not fall for the same amount of time, and everything there will become poisonous. In the Mahabharata, Arjuna and Ashwatthama used the Brahmashira against each other. Fearing that the power of these two astras would destroy the world, the sages beseeched the two warriors to take back their weapons

Stories of advanced shapeshifting reptilians are in fables, myth and culture all over the world. In Scottish faerie tales the 'blue men of the minches' [R Kirk] or the (water dwelling) 'Draco' and the weapons of great power brought to the Celtic shores by the incoming gods of reptilian dynasty .. e.g. the spear of Lugh, the sword Excalibur etc.

The purana also points to the association of the cult of Nagas with that of Shiva. In the Mahabharata and Harivamsa texts, Shesha was considered the son of Shiva. A lesser relation was developed with regard to Vishnu as in his sheshashayi form which links the primal waters with the sleeping Vishnu.

Mme. H. P. Blavatsky [fl. 1900] co-founder of the Theosophical Society, thought:

When the Brahmans invaded India they "found a race of wise men, half-gods, half-demons", says the legend, men who were the teachers of other races and became likewise the instructors of the Hindus and the Brahmans themselves.

THE WARM POLAR REGIONS OF THE EARTH

Amongst humanity that is 'not in the know' or on a 'need to know' basis there is some evidence apparent that the world really isn't everything we have been told it is - it is in fact far more than that !!

By Lieutenant-Commander Fitzhugh Green, U.S.N. (c.a. 1914)

'In the proposed transpolar flight of the huge new navy dirigible, the ZR-1 (the Shenandoah), next summer, lies the most thrilling possibility that ever faced a single body of explorers;

In the centre of the unknown area of the Polar Sea may be discovered a vast continent heated by subterranean fires, and inhabited by the descendants of the last Norwegian colony of Greenland!

So wild is the idea as to tax the most gullible imagination. Yet it is vividly encouraged and supported not only by history and tradition, but by the searching test of scientific analysis...'

Examine the Eskimo tradition: It paints in vivid terms the White Men swarming suddenly north to a wonderland the natives long had known. Because of evil spirits, no Eskimo had ever dared this trail.

'Confirming that the earth is indeed hollow, in February 19, 1947, Admiral Richard E. Byrd of the United States Navy flew north from Alaska beyond the north pole on a flight of 1700 miles over the Arctic Ocean and came to a land covered with vegetation, lakes and rivers and even saw a prehistoric-type mammoth in the underbrush.

From his allegedly suppressed but now available diary, an entry of the flight log:

https://www.bibliotecapleyades.net/tierra_hueca/esp_tierra_hueca_2d.htm

At 0910 Hours - Both Magnetic and Gyro compasses beginning to gyrate and wobble, we are unable to hold our heading by instrumentation. Take bearing with Sun compass, yet all seems well. The controls are seemingly slow to respond and have sluggish quality, but there is no indication of Icing!

At 1135 Hours- Our radio crackles and a voice comes through in English with what perhaps is a slight Nordic or Germanic accent! The message is:

'Welcome, Admiral, to our domain. We shall land you in exactly seven minutes! Relax, Admiral, you are in good hands.'

This point is corroborated by the author of "The Arctic World" who says the same thing about the aurora. Moreover, William Denovan in his scientific reference work, "The Phenomena of Nature", makes the statement that:

"In temperate regions the aurora does not present such grand forms as in the extreme north."

Observations by north polar explorers indicate that there is indeed a land in the far north with a subtropical climate heated by a sister sun inside Our Hollow Earth. For example, Explorer's reports of abundant animal and bird life in the summer time in the far north indicates a homeland in the north from which they extend in the summer further south and to which they are seen to migrate in the fall.

With something simple such as the interplay of light causing issues with public domain science and its opportunity to verify a hidden structure to our planet, perhaps evidence for very unexpected geological realities and strata can be found in the evident biology ?
Explorer Hays observed abundant insect life in the far north. When he was in latitude 78 degrees, 17 minutes in early July he said, "I secured a yellow-winged butterfly, and-who would believe it--a mosquito...ten moths, three spiders, two bees and two flies." (The Open Polar Sea, p. 413)

Notice the element of surprise that many explorers expressed resulting from the discovery of conditions which they weren't expecting.

Explorer Greely, in his book, THREE YEARS OF ARCTIC SERVICE, in Grinnell Land in June of 1881, reports birds of an unknown species, butterflies and bumblebees, so many flies they couldn't sleep at night, and temperatures of 47 and 50 degrees at latitude 81 degrees 49 minutes north. He also found plenty willow to make fire, and much driftwood, (Chapter 26, Vol. I)

A Swedish expedition under Otto Torell, found near Trurenberg Bay in the Arctic Sea, trees floating with green buds on them and among them was found the seed of the tropical Entada Bean which measured 2.25 inches across. (Gardner, p. 253)

Explorer Sverdrup at 81 degrees north found so many hares that they named one inlet, Hare Fiord. Also nearly all expedition parties found enough game to keep their exploring parties well fed with meat. These included herds of musk-oxen and reindeer. (Gardner p. 254)

Captain Beechey saw so many birds on the west coast of Spitzbergen that sometimes a single shot killed thirty of them. (Gardner p. 254)

All explorers observed that not all animals migrate south to escape the cold Arctic winds in winter, but many instead go north. Where do they go? Greely, surprised at the tremendous amount of wildlife in a supposed frozen north wrote, "Surely this presence of birds and flowers and beasts was a greeting on nature's part to our new home."

Explorer Kane reported seeing several groups of Brent Geese, which is an American migratory bird, flying NORTHEAST in their wedge-shaped line of flight at 80 degrees 50' north at Cape Jackson, near Grinnelland in late June 1854.

Explorer Greely makes this statement of the northward migration of bears, "Lieutenant Lockwood, in May, 1882, noticed bear tracks (going northeast) on the north coast of Greenland, near Cape Bennet in 83 degrees 3' N.," and commented, "...I cannot understand why the bear ever leaves the rich hunting-field of the 'North Water' for the desolate shores of the northward." (THREE YEARS, p. 366)

◆ ◆ ◆

THE 'ANCIENT' GUARDIANS OF LOCAL VOODOO IN SCOTLAND

Jeremiah 10:11 Thus shall ye say unto them, The gods that have not made the heavens and the earth, even they shall perish from the earth, and from under these heavens.

At one time - amongst the ancient mountains and woods of Scotland, no doubt the 'men of renown' - the giant races mentioned in the Bible, in this neck of the woods called the 'Fomorians' [c.f. painter and colourist John Duncan of Dundee. early 1900's] were interacting with and impressing the natives.

image: 'the Fomorians' by Celtic revivalist painter John Duncan - the 'unseelie court'

With many references in Folklore [MM Banks, Carmichael, Kirk etc also at www.sacredtexts] we can hear stories of the 'fishy' sounding 'Draco' or 'Blue (aquatic) Men of the Minches', or of towns like Glasgow named after their blue pallour, e.g. 'Glae' or even paint ourselves blue with 'woad' to attempt to draw on and emulate their 'magical' powers and martial prowess.

image: a giant stone doorway about 20 metres high, Glencoe, Scotland.

An ancient, human-looking, but actually non-human people calling themselves Druids and said by e.g. Masonic historian George Oliver to be worshipping the serpent god Hu and certainly carving images of serpents into the local standing stones seemed to move with the times - eventually masters of computer-aided designs and city architecture plans.

image: alleged Bronze-Age carving of Reptilian on the 'spirit rock', by the North Esk river at Rosslyn, Scotland.

Local Lore tells its own stories

With folklore (Kirk, 1697) replete with a menagerie or a *'secret commonwealth'* of beings of all shapes, sizes and scales it was possible in the 20th century to look in the Parish records of the Isle of Skye to find out how the local non-humans were voting in village disputes in the 17th Century. [O'Keefe].

According to the O'Clerys 'Book of Invasions', 1631, an old Celtic work, and also in the mythology of the Celtic gods, the Kings of this giant and equipped race arrived on these outer shores of Western Europe after an ancient war bringing with them powerful artefacts such as the cup, the lance and the sword of destiny. The Lance of Lugh in most accounts sounds like a devastating laser blaster - whilst the magical sword is one we tend to equate with the mythical Arthurian sword of power Excalibur. In some accounts the race of the De Dannan are fallen angels, [Walking the Faery Pathway, p67, Harmonia Saille], who decided to stay underground after defeat by the Milesians.

e.g. In Ireland there were a group of giant warriors called the Fir Bolg Knights. The records suggest that they were initially enslaved by the Greeks and made to carry bags of soil or clay, hence the name 'Fir Bolg' (men of bags) but eventually returned to Ireland - where they were eventually defeated by the artefact wielding and sorcerous 'Tuatha De Dannan'.

"At Brefy, in the Co. of Mayo, A.D. 1732, in a coffin, inscribed in Irish characters, the coffin of Genan, which contained a skeleton, 12.5 feet long. Genan was King of Ireland, 'A.M. 3352, P.D. 7024, A.C. 1781' and this monument is erected (at Castlebar church) *to show the antiquity of the Irish character and the size of menkind in those early ages, A.D. I756."*

The Celtic fringes of Europe appear to be full of stories of otherworldly people.

However from the 17th century writings of the Reverend Kirk we hear tales of the Blue Men of the Minches, aquatic beings who stayed in Scottish waters off the Inner Hebrides and from Campbell's 'Superstitions', we hear of the 18th century sect of shapeshifters on the Isle of Lewis in Scotland called the 'MacCodrums of the Seal'. Beings that fitted the description of the shapeshifting sumerian anunnaki - aka the De Dannan then were historically deployed amongst the surface geography of the Celtic and Pictish world. Small wonder therefore that the ancient tribes of humans e.g. the Picts who lived on the land in Scotland would paint themselves blue with woad to attempt to resonate with, draw from and acquire the god-like prowess of this race in battle.

PINING FOR CHANGE

There is some tenuous historic and cultural evidence for the behind-the-human-scenes magic use from these beings. The sort of thing that would make them consultants to kings and tribes, using powers of 'magic' to favour some and disfavour others.

e.g. the use of magic 'voodoo' directed at or drawn from natural, abundant objects - carvings of; pollen grains - (Pine, grass etc), virus, spores or small creatures with the capacity to regenerate from the most disrupted states.

When we look at the morphology of common Scottish pollen grains, the male gamete in plant reproduction, we discover the very striking similarities of these stone carved objects to the pollen of local plant species such as; Scots Pine and Grass. It's understandable that the museum archaeologists cannot publish a full explanation of these artefacts and the uses to which they were put.

image: mysterious 'religious artefacts' as modern art, Festival square, Edinburgh, Scotland.

Given what is accepted about our own pre-history our records do not credit primitive tribes living in Scotland with the technology to magnify pollen, fungal spores or virus capsules to such an extent that accurate three-dimensional stone models could be carved of them. There are only two possibilities.

1. either Bronze Age Scotland had microscopes and technological infrastructure, or,

2. some people in Bronze Age Scotland had paranormal powers of sight, special knowledge, or non-human tools.

Given the 'primitive painted savages' theme that we have inherited from historical BC accounts, it does seem unlikely that the ancient Picts invented microscopy beating the 16th Century Dutch to the draw.

The use of Paranormal vision, knowledge and or non-human tools therefore is likely.

WHERE DID SUCH STUFF COME FROM ?

A recently declassified CIA Document on Catastrophic Earth Changes: CIA-RDP79B00752A000300070001-8, by Thomas Chan speaks of a burgeoning tropical population in Alaska and Siberia suddenly wiped out - and of frozen mammoths with mouths full of buttercups, coral reefs under the Arctic etc

Scotland and the UK disconnected from western mainland

Europe when the lowlands of Doggerland were inundated and sank after the Tsunami generated by a very massive landslip off the Norwegian cost called the Storegga Slides, approximately 6200BC. We also know from Michael Cremo's 'Forbidden Archaeology, 2001' of very ancient *hi-tek* finds in strata from distant epochs.
Is there another factor at play amongst the primitive Scottish tribes ? Perhaps a hidden race of shapeshifting reptilian beings that had - or indeed still have - the special abilities to see and utilise such occult realities?

Indeed given the high-tech mythology of the alleged Reptilian underworlds such as the Tibetan Nagaland, or Shamballah, were some of these special Druids also using ancient iPads ?

FINDING A SYMPATHETIC DRUID

Given that the stone-carved; pollen-grains, protozoa, spore and virus models are officially classified as 'religious artefacts' could they be used to sympathetically resonate with and draw power from or even mis-direct the generative processes of the plants etc. they represent during the growing season? Druids practising such sympathetic magic would indeed be, like Merlin - 'one with the land', drawing of its power. See Sir James Fraser's study of ancient beliefs 'The Golden Bough', 1922, chapter 3 Sympathetic Magic

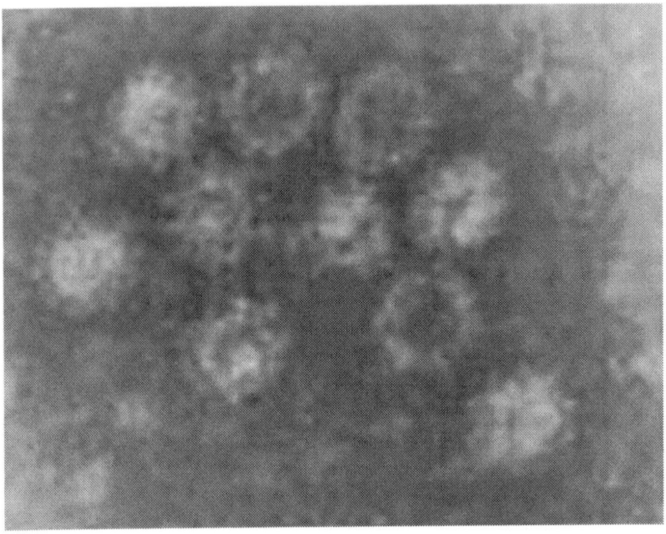

Drawing from energy lines only they could see or feel during solstice or equinox, or lunar tidal energies using appropriate seasonal foci e.g. grass or pine pollen during the summer or healing from the burgeoning paramecium protozoa population by use of handheld sympathetic model, or by misdirecting fungal growth to infest the grain harvest of the human 'enemy' etc it can't be said that things were entirely negative.

For absolute certain though, latter day folklore collectors like Carmichael collected tales of the Hebrides and the crofting communities showing them to be in an endless battle for their very souls against some persistent demonic-sounding deceit and malevolence. It does appear that that dark side of what becomes modern

SCOTTISH 'FARMING'

Scotland fully embraced these dark fate-filled illusions, powers and principalities for millennia. The Kelpies monument near Falkirk appears consistent with this idea but somehow incongruous at night - lit up in eerie-looking lights.

The Kelpies are a name borrowed from dark abducting faeries from the West Highland Sea Lochs. According to the Sculptor, Andy Scott, "The artistic intent (of the Kelpies) is built around a contemporary sculptural monument. Water-borne, towering gateways into The Helix, the Forth & Clyde canal and Scotland, translating the legacy of the area into proud equine guardians."

With perhaps the final Scottish harvest in mind, our possible soul-farmers and their stealthy allies appear to be deploying all sorts of 'netting' around the lives of their alleged livestock.

Yet, there are other forces and influences at work in this same part of Scotland. Within 10 miles of this monument is the Falkirk UFO Triangle, with its alien-looking activity. At Bonnybridge, UFO's seem quieter these days but then there is plenty of *hi-tek* phone masts. Are these new communications technologies a prelude to more 'space-age' *hi-tek* voodoo ??

Since the early 1930's the alleged coming world religion of scientific humanism by applications within a radio-wave environment was initially known as 'radio-eugenics' [Karl Reisner] and as Drew Hempel illustrates it then became the modern Transhuman movement.

It is true to say that most of the young today can usually be found with their necks bent downward operating some APP on a handheld device.

Are the reptilian druids of today working computers and IT ?

Whilst nearer Edinburgh at Gorebridge - evidence of un-human nonsense is as highly strange as usual and ever-present.

THE END OF HEROES

image: alien-looking creature on the roof at Gorebridge

The slaying of the Christian King, Arthur by the pagan faction led by Mordred near Stirling c.a. 150AD ended with a big symbolic stone beehive built over the spot at Camelon, according to the ancient historian Nennius. Unlucky for the ancient Knights of the Round Table, but not for purchasers of Lottery tickets in the 20th Century - as the number of lucky, life-changing Lottery wins has caused the 'UFO Triangle' to be called the 'Golden Circle' !

The veneration of what is not good continues though.

The beehive is a probable reference not just to the veneration of the insect and its 'Platonic caste system', but to the biblical prophesy enacted by Samson on finding a wild beehive inside a

lion he slew with his bare
hands .. '*out of the strong comes forth the sweet*' - to some this comes to mean 'making heaven on earth by cooperation and industry out of the dead opportunities and bodies of the Christian or Davidic line (symbolised by the lion of David).

This, ongoing, historic, so-called 'Merovingian conspiracy', allegedly enacted by the lost or wandering and pantheistic tribe of Dan, descendants of biblical (disinherited) Esau was all about diminishing Christianity - the descendants of Jacob.

Clearly though, behind the interdimensional and heavenly scenes, for centuries after Arthur fell, incoming Celtic Saints; Fillan, Mungo, Patrick, Margaret, Cuthbert etc ... then the risen St Andrew and heavenly Angels [up to Athelstaneford 832AD] .... produced miracle after astounding miracle in their battle for the souls of Scotland.

e.g. the mysterious teleporting arm-bone. or mane, of St Fillan that re-appeared from a distant casket to assist Scottish hopes to win at Bannockburn in 1314AD

(images: Rosslyn Chapel and below, St Fillan's Holy Pool)

(Picture: the Scottish miracle in the clouds over Athelstanefored battlefield, morning, 823AD)

Even the Most High sends an Angel in a dream to St Regulus telling him to take the bones of St Andrew from the then centre of ancient civilisation to 'the ends of the earth' - and he then gets shipwrecked in Fife, Scotland. Up against powerful shape-shifting 'tricksters' though, who always seemed one step ahead either in battle, technology, or insight - the early Scottish humanity seemed hard-pressed to discover which ritual stones or alignments to stars, planets, moons, heights or depths, if any, were going to deliver them.

Indeed, some of the human Seers in the Scottish Highlands such as the Brahan Seer discovered their 'gift' had a dark and morbid fascination. e.g. 13th Century Thomas of Ercildoune who prophesised about the early 14th Century battle at Bannockburn; *'the burn o' breid shall be dunged wi deid'* - i.e. the dead shall fill thc bannock (bread) burn.

(Picture the view from Bannockburn, and Bruce Memorial to Cambusbarron - area of recent 'high strangeness')

Whereas Scottish victory at Bannockburn may have been ordained by God through St Fillan, it is a decisive battle that darkness, never-the-less appears to claw back its losses from; whether in the 13th Century Rhymer prophesies about the battle with its morbid vision of destiny, or in more recent 20th Century allusions.

image: Luciferic symbolism adorning Scottish flagpole at Bannockburn, Scotland.

Depending on the level of sacrifice to and appeasement of the powers - for some, the seasonal calendar and its customs [British Calendar Customs, MM Banks, 1931 vol. 1-3, 4] fulfilled all social needs and hopes. It was always true that things could only get better! Folklore has offerings of porridge to gods of the sea in the Hebrides and modern Scotland has monuments to the gods and godesses of nature. Indeed some of the ancient bonefire celebrations were, literally that. Banks in her research hears of the story where the old are thrown on the bonefires of Halloween like 'cords of wood'.

KEEPING THE TRADITIONS

Near the churchyard at Sound, Weisdale on the mainland of the Shetland Islands, are the foundations of a pre-Reformation Chapel called the Aamos Kirk.

What follows is another example of the battle of Light versus Darkness for the souls of Scotland.

The landowner had a dream to donate the land for the church, and during its construction, at the end of the day when the builders had run out of stone, there was always a fresh supply of materials in the morning. Folks also noticed the presence of one extra builder that could not be accounted for during the construction. Throughout the centuries the Aamos Kirk has been a site of good-intentioned miracles, prayers and wishes. Today though with its baptismal font displaced into other practises in the surrounding trees and with the placement of one or two ethnic-looking monuments it does seem to be in a post-Christian epoch.

The local C21st. monuments to such elemental 'powers' in Shetland depict people of 'blue-green' disposition that are 'of the sea'.

Such was the obvious renown of and fear of those with magical powers who could summon such elemental forces [e.g. (Scottish) King Arthur's Merlin, C2nd, Nobles; Hugh de Giffard C12th and Sir Michael Scott C13th], that the counsel, strategies and solutions, influence and spells of Druidic Mages were probably a 'must have' for those in need.
The photo depicts a 'green man' aka Cernunnos/Baal near Bannockburn, also near to where King Arthur was slain at Camelon.

In East Lothian, at Yester Castle, it was locally told that the black Mage Hugh De Giffard summoned demons to build his castle, and in Kirkcaldy, Fife, dread deeds of magic were according to the stories regularly enacted by the Mage Michael Scott - who having employed the devil to do construction of his roads and castle, apparently gave it the further job of making an eternal rope out of the sands of Kirkcaldy beach.

image: Balwearie castle, Kirkcaldy, belonging to Sir Michael Scott

That after allegedly being conveyed in the air as a Scottish ambassador to the French Court to end piracy on Scottish trading ships with a demonstration and threat of seismic events summoned at will.

◆ ◆ ◆

LOOKING FURTHER INTO THINGS

Probable evidence of the non-human reality of some Druids has survived and is currently preserved by the National Museum of Scotland in Chambers Street, Edinburgh and on display in the '0' lower level of the Hawthornden building.

In the display cabinet are stone-carved objects the size of tennis balls with regular protrusions and furrows on them, some spherical, some with patterns, some elongated - they are simply noted as religious artefacts found at ancient stone circles with no other explanation given as to their meaning or use. In legends and myths attributed to the Druids and Merlin from Sir Thomas Malory's Le Morte D'Arthur of romance tales about the legendary King Arthur, from 1485, we hear that the Druid Merlin is 'one with the land'. Perhaps these small stone artefacts in the National Museum of Scotland give us a strong clue as to how that can be.

The same architects of stone circles and their energy dynamics, who were incredible athletes and warriors, also understood the powers of resonance and harmony and disharmony and disease.

e.g. The local landscape was walked and dowsed in Perthshire hills, [Cowan. D, c.a. 1985], and the flat table-like cup-marked stones with hollows showing energy sinks in the local land, are shown to be a topographical local energy map showing ley-line contours. ???

One of the central Masonic writers notes a connection between Serpent lore and the Druids. *"The Druids had a high veneration for the Serpent. Their great god, Hu, was typified by that reptile; and he is represented by the Bards as 'the wonderful chief Dragon, the sovereign of heaven'."* George Oliver, Signs and Symbols, New York, Macoy Publishing and Masonic Supply Company, 1906, p. 36

image: Dragon carving of dynastic nature near Stirling Bridge - site of an important Scottish battle and victory in 1297AD.

The inference to be drawn from the Edinburgh National museum display is that in ancient and perhaps modern times there were and are people who had special powers of sight operating a paradigm of hidden energies and the mechanics of sympathetic magic on a Harry Potteresque scale. In the more recent centuries an occult sub-culture of energy forms and mechanics invisible to the ordinary human being have become apparent from the writings of Emmanuel Swedenborg circa. 1760, and also from Theosophy, a body of Eastern mystical teaching founded by HP Blavatsky in 1875. Theosophist CW Leadbeater writes of the mechanics of energy absorption he was witnessing in 'The Hidden Side of Things', 1913,

114. THE ABSORPTION OF VITALITY This vitality is absorbed by all living organisms, and a sufficient supply of it seems to be a necessity of their existence. In the case of men and the higher animals it is absorbed through the centre or vortex in the etheric double which corresponds with the spleen. It will be remembered that that centre has six petals, made by the undulatory movement of the forces which cause the vortex ...

116. When the unit of vitality is flashing about in the atmosphere, brilliant as it is, it is almost colourless, and may be compared to white light. But as soon as it is drawn into the vortex of the force-centre at the spleen it is decomposed and breaks up into streams of different colours ... Those rays then rush off in different directions, each to do its special work in the vitalisation of the body.

Perhaps the secret schools and secret beings of old taught ways to acquire and use these energies. What modern social artefacts would be used by these beings today to draw generative essences and life-force from ?
The glowing or shining ones, the reptilian illuminati see each other amongst the human parade very easily with their all-seeing eyes. There is today a large volume of secret literature that venerates the light-filled serpent.

"The serpent is the symbol and prototype of the Universal Savior, who redeems the worlds by giving creation the knowledge of itself and the realization of good and evil." Manly P. Hall, 33 Degree Mason, The Secret Teachings of All Ages, 1928
It does seem that however many apples of knowledge we get handed these days they are not leading us to completion in important areas such as physics or medicine or interstellar transport !

We hear from the near East from 'The History of the Jews' by Josephus Flavius in 584BC, [published Murray, London, 1839] of the fallen angels e.g 'Tubalcain', who would teach man artifice. As we can perhaps see today from the paradigm of magical feeding on display outside the Sheraton hotel in Edinburgh, perhaps the shapeshifting reptilian gods of Sumeria are still busy.

Unfortunately, of the apples of alleged knowledge we may be tempted with today, none of those fallen arts are the arts of free energy and self-sufficiency for the race of Adam.. Given there appears to be many different types of 'human impersonation' underway .. perhaps in passing it can be observed that death, birth and this dimension may not always live up to human or Draconian perspectives. The human deals with being hatched, matched, taxed and dispatched and with all the 'noble' lies in-between, whilst it may be that our human looking Reptilians and some of these other species see reasons to be very different from humanity.

Given the things that they can see - perhaps given their innate capacity to be superb toolusers, musicians and controllers, inventors, fighters and healers, architects and artists etc they choose not to farm humanity in a sleepy Sci-Fi Utopia.

Preferring instead, Pyramids and sandcastles being constantly washed away by the tides of time.

All over this planet, and indeed others in the solar system - the ancient pyramid builders have been at work.

e.g. A feathered serpent deity has been worshiped by many different ethnopolitical groups in Mesoamerican history.

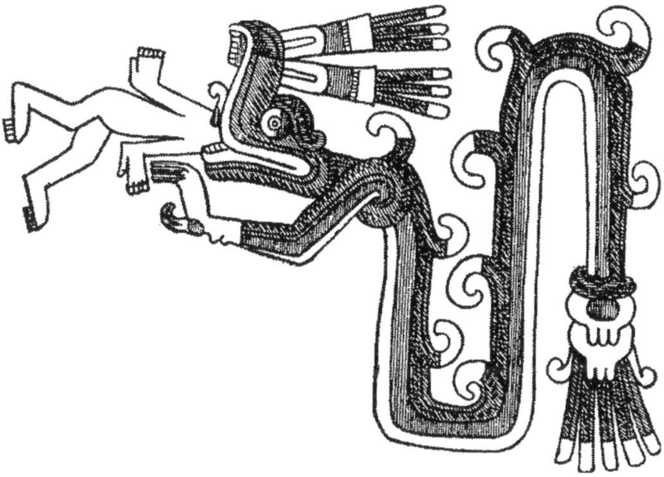

image: Quetzalcoatl, Mayan Reptilian Diety, South America

THE HOST WITH THE MOST

Perhaps happy that humanity is full of pretensions to want to be at least as good at doing things the way the Reptilians can .. some of humanity wear the 'emperor's clothes' or 'souls-netting' [i.e. investments in physical superiority] every chance they get - the Reptilians/Overlords then feel justified to insert and then gestate some 'little emperors' of their own!

'Symbiosis is an umbrella term referring to any long-term interaction between two organisms that share a close physical space.

Symbiosis is broken down into mutualism, commensalism, and parasitism based on how two species interact in their ecosystem. Mutualism is where both organisms benefit, commensalism is where one benefits but the other organism isn't harmed, and lastly, parasitism is where one organism benefits and the other is harmed'.

[www. sciencetrends .com]

Given the Gnostic terminology taught to refer to such 'occult hosting events' for the human in various states of 'being' e.g.

Hrumachis, Phoenix, then one might be led to assume that the Draconian-Human symbiosis of soul is ultimately a parasitic one.

Getting hosted and then used as an 'occult' incubator in this love-in isn't probably what most human beings would want.

Moreover, there does appear to be a body of literature e.g. Theosophy, that supports this next 19th Century illustration.

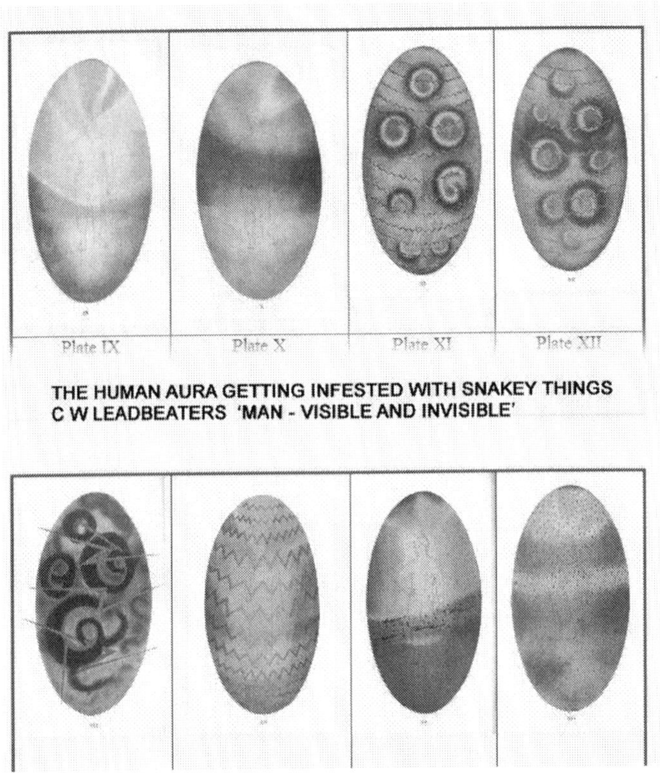

THE HUMAN AURA GETTING INFESTED WITH SNAKEY THINGS
C W LEADBEATERS 'MAN - VISIBLE AND INVISIBLE'

THE HIDDEN HAND

It may be fair to assume that mankind has been generally unaware of those amongst us with special powers. Perhaps humanity ridden with dented pride and envy has been unable to recognise or acknowledge these feats of incredible genius when first seen - or rather perhaps there is nowhere to go with the story - for the all-seeing eye sees all etc

COMING OUT IN SYMPATHY

Sympathetic resonance or sympathetic vibration is a harmonic phenomenon wherein a formerly passive string or vibratory body responds to external vibrations to which it has a harmonic likeness.

The mechanics of resonance were well understood in ancient times, indeed it is alleged that many huge buildings e.g in Egypt were erected by using focussed sound resonance to levitate and move massive weights, or in modern times, the Coral Castle in Florida during the mid-20th Century.

The classic example is demonstrated with two similar tuning-forks of which one is mounted on a wooden box. If the other one is struck and then placed on the box, then muted, the unstruck mounted fork will be heard. Similarly face two identically tuned acoustic guitars to each other, strum one and the other guitar will be heard vibrating.

It is clear from the evidence that some would end up seeking the voodoo of the druids, and not just would-be Kings, Queens and Princes but those local farmers in East and Northern Scotland who wanted to use that extra stealth and hidden advantage over their commercial or military rivals.

The conversation, probably on some full electromagnetic and tidal moon at a stone circle carefully surveyed by some occult process unknown to humans and put there to focus the emerging power of the land on this particular evening at one central seat or point - probably starts by approaching the Druid with some offerings and a suitable petition.

The Druid, using the surge of tidal moon energies as booster, may have been refreshing himself/herself with one or two of the plant pollen artifacts in their hands, drawing on and drinking in the generative powers of growth e.g. from local pine trees or some grain crop. The Spring and growing season now underway and the air laden with pollen, some empathetic surge of power from the land and its new growth is perhaps in order after a dark and cold winter. He puts down the sympathetically resonant stone-carved models of tetraporate or tetracolpate pollen, or saccate pollen from e.g. pine or grass. He can also call on spir-aperturate pollen to grow amongst diseased crops to harden the surviving plants to their newly extreme environments. From the usual tale of human woe the Druid decides how to assist the humans. e.g. he/she opens up a small cave/receptacle under the central altar stone and then brings out some very strange and curious handheld and stone-carved objects. To date, many of these have been discovered on pagan religious sites/circles up the fertile north east coastland of the old Pictish Kingdoms.

Some folks say they are fishing weights, or a curious game, or a badge with which to enter a secret club or guild - but that's to the untrained eye.

Back to our story .. choices, choices - firstly he asks .. do you want your neighbour to be healed of their ailments, rejuvenated ??? and then he holds up for all to see a scale model stone carving of a Paramecium, an invasive single-celled micro-organism 0.05 to 0.32 mm.

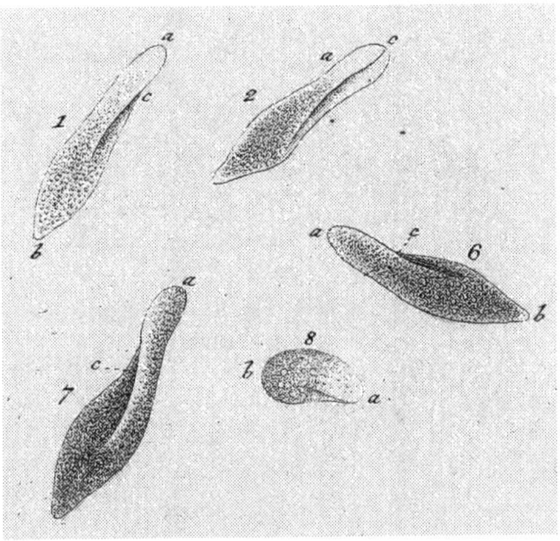

The Paramecium was allegedly first discovered and named and drawn in the 17th Century, but thousands of years ago - somehow - it appeared to have been carved out and modelled in stone as a rejuvenating and self-healing, sacred creature upon whose energies to draw in times of physical need.

e.g. *'The power to regenerate is ... an indication of the vitality of the individual cell..'* [Peebles, F. 'REGENERATION AND REGULATION IN PARAMECIUM CAUDATUM', 1910.]

How then, thousands of years ago in the cold, wet and barbarian climate of ancient Scotland could such a detailed and revealing study be made of the physiology and life-cycle of this creature - to be able to study, draw and carve this object to scale having evaluated and discerned its capacity to rejuvenate ? To then produce models of objects that are mere nanometres e.g. virus capsules, or micrometers suggests a highly advanced or beyond the human, visioning system ...

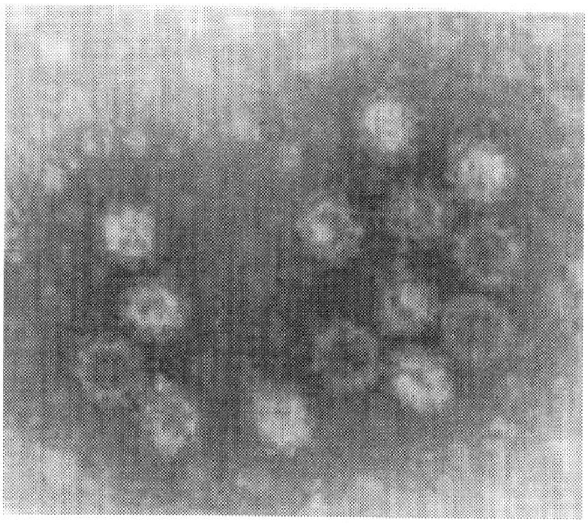

.. Or worse ! declares the Druid .. do your rivals need some diarrhea ?? and pulls out a weighty stone carving of an Enterovirus - beyond the capacity of a good optical microscope to envision at some 30nm Or, he smiles, we could lighten up and blight their barley with some stem rot - then holds up a knobbly looking fungal spore,
e.g. Aspergillus Niger

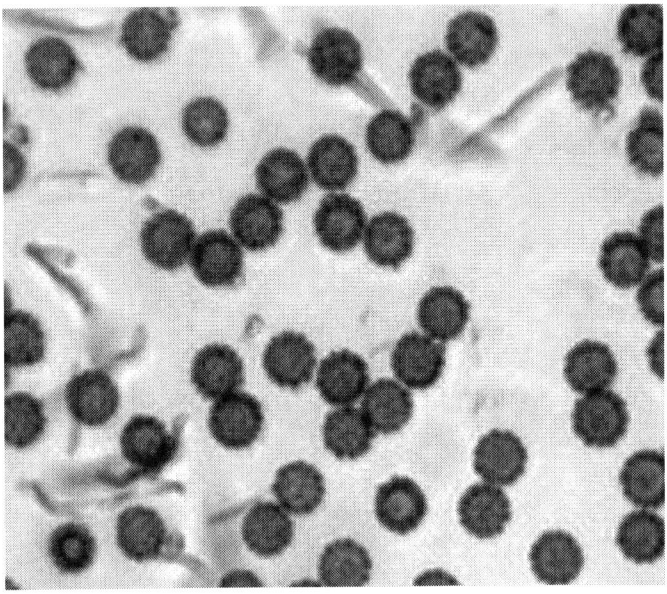

or, he smiles, their crops wont be the same after this and holds up a stone carved scale model of a club-like fungal fruiting body about 6um called a 'basidium'. A small structure, shaped like a club, found in the Basidiomycota division of fungi, that bears four spores at the tips of small projections.

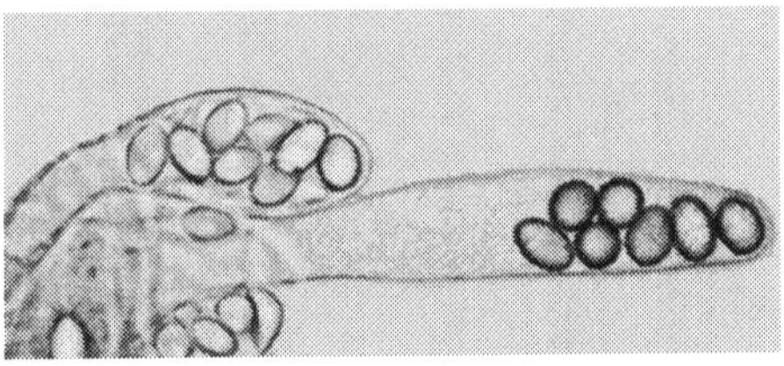

and, or for a bit of fun we could infest their cattle, dogs and sheep with these - he holds up a stone carved model of a hungry looking hard shelled tick with its wrinkly skin having the 'festoons' - [i.e. a network of hard supports to hold the expanding blood sac.] needed to store lots of blood .. after its bite.

Ixodes ricinus, the castor bean tick, is a chiefly European species of hard-bodied tick. It may reach a length of 11 mm (0.43 in) when engorged with a blood meal, and can transmit both bacterial and viral pathogens such as the causative agents of Lyme disease and tick-borne encephalitis. The secondary infections (like Lyme Disease) could wear them down eventually ...

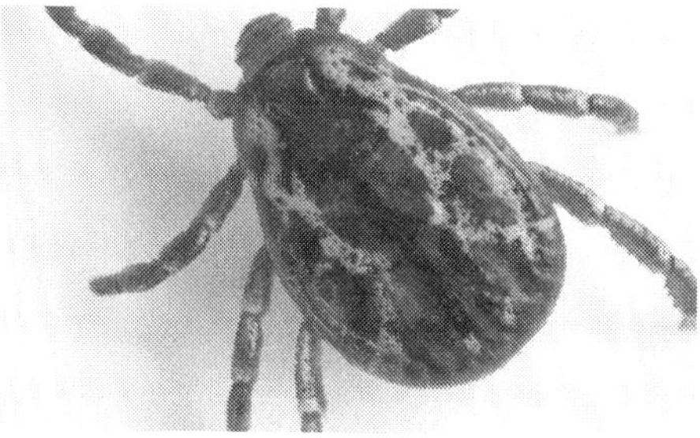

Alternatively .. one could send in the weevils during the summer or near harvest ..

The important wingless weevils in the UK are members of the beetle group belonging to the genus Otiorhynchus. Within this genus at least three are important pests of soft fruit in the UK. They are the vine weevil (Otiorhynchus sulcatus), clay-coloured weevil (O. singularis) and the strawberry weevil (O. ovatus). The first two weevils are particularly important in northern Britain amongst native berry crops.

ARCHITECTS OF HUMAN DISTRESS ?

What then do our Anu-nnaki Voodoo Non-humans do in the 21st Century with their shining in the dark, illuminated super-abilities ? Designing and implementing a building that looks like the inside of a snakes head for the Pope to sit in whilst giving a reception or audience in Vatican City. Or,

Still constructing voodoo cities and angular and enumerated street plans to help harvest energies using scale models ? Or Perhaps on a global scale, building cities and structures from as far apart as; London - England, Washington DC, Astana in Kazakstan, or Canberra in Australia, or even in Edinburgh - Scotland there is a grand scale of numerology and energy harvesting at work. Draconian Draco, Dragons and the Anu, the Anunnaki and Danu - where they really live, host and reproduce is open to debate !

The inference to be drawn from the museum display of handheld stone carvings found on ancient religious sites, is that in ancient and perhaps modern times there were and are people who had special powers of sight operating with a paradigm of hidden energies and the mechanics of sympathetic magic on a Harry Potteresque scale.

In the more recent centuries an occult sub-culture of energy forms and mechanics invisible to the ordinary human being have become apparent from the writings of Emmanuel Swedenborg circa. 1760, and also from Theosophy, a body of Eastern mystical teaching founded by HP Blavatsky in 1875.

Theosophist CW Leadbeater writes of the mechanics of energy absorption he was witnessing in 'The Hidden Side of Things', 1913,

114. THE ABSORPTION OF VITALITY This vitality is absorbed by all living organisms, and a sufficient supply of it seems to be a necessity of their existence. In the case of men and the higher animals it is absorbed through the centre or vortex in the etheric double which corresponds with the spleen. It will be remembered that that centre has six petals, made by the undulatory movement of the forces which cause the vortex ...

116. When the unit of vitality is flashing about in the atmosphere, brilliant as it is, it is almost colourless, and may be compared to white light. But as soon as it is drawn into the vortex of the force-centre at the spleen it is decomposed and breaks up into streams of different colours ... Those rays then rush off in different directions, each to do its special work in the vitalisation of the body.

Perhaps the secret schools and secret beings of old taught ways to acquire and use these energies. We can see the Luciferian (snake emblem) Theosophical Society goals of the new Matraiya etc and Space Masters emerging today - but at the back of it all is the central set of assumptions that cement the hierarchy together.

Hard Brains equals a hard life ?

The following quotes are from an Esoteric Section publication - part of the secret organisation with many Objectives that runs the more ecumenical sounding ordinary Theosophical Society [Exoteric Society] with its Three (more sensible) Objects.

The Esoteric Section: Morals and beliefs published [circa 1960]

P97 GS Arundale: the whole object of the Esoteric School is to lead you from the world of men into the world of the masters, and you must take as your standard the morality of the masters and not that of the world.

P161 Sri Ram '... the changes they are planning for the world'

P151 A Besant 'Then came the need for the great shaking, when elements had accumulated that were not ready to go further. It had to be a very great shaking, for the times demanded it, in order that the advance afterwards might be rapid. This time it came [in 1907], all the turmoil and its inevitable results in shaking out a large number of good and earnest people who were nevertheless no good to us at the moment because they could not adapt themselves to the new life.

P121 Jinarajadasa '.. the Lords of karma may put you in a race that has no tendency to occultism - you may possibly get a hard brain so that you will not be able to meditate.

P25 A Besant '.. you have to learn to make the mind sensitive to orders that come to you from the Higher Mind, and then you gradually get the feeling that your mind is not you, but something for use ... the drudgery has to be done until the mind becomes automatically obedient.

P37 A Besant '.. I cannot imagine anyone who is a disciple doing anything but obeying without cavil or delay any order that comes from his superior.'

P35 A Besant '.. the Hierarchy - has no break therin; it is because any command which is given comes down from grade to grade, and grade to grade until it reaches the disciple appointed.'

P50 Jinarajadasa 'take the case of the member who comes into this school. He is presumably sincere, he has read certain rules, and he signs a promise or a pledge. No-one has compelled him to come in, and he knows exactly to what he is subscribing. If after subscribing to the rules of the esoteric school he voluntarily, to suit his own convenience, adopts modifications of them, it is obvious that he is not playing the game.

P156 N Sri Ram '.. members [of the ES] to act as a definite instrument through which the hierarchy can act upon the Society..'

P127 HPB The Theosophist Aug 1931. 'The Esoteric Section is thus 'set apart' for the salvation of the whole Society.

What modern social artefacts would be used by these beings today to draw generative essences and life-force from ? The glowing or shining ones, the reptilian illuminati see each other amongst the human parade very easily with their all-seeing eyes.

The scales of ones local problem

There is today a large volume of secret literature that venerates the light-filled serpent.

"The serpent is the symbol and prototype of the Universal Savior, who redeems the worlds by giving creation the knowledge of itself and the realization of good and evil." Manly P. Hall, 33 Degree Mason, The Secret Teachings of All Ages, 1928

It does seem that however many apples of knowledge we get handed these days they are not leading us to completion in important areas such as physics or medicine or interstellar transport!
We hear from the near East from 'The History of the Jews' by Josephus Flavius in 584BC, [published Murray, London, 1839] of the fallen angels e.g. Samael, who would teach man artifice.

As we can perhaps see today from the paradigm of magical feeding on display outside the Sheraton hotel in Edinburgh, perhaps the shape-shifting reptilian gods of Sumeria are still busy. Unfortunately, of the apples of alleged knowledge we may be tempted with today, none of those fallen arts are the arts of free energy and self-sufficiency for the race of Adam.. It may be fair to assume that mankind has been generally unaware of those amongst us with special powers.

Perhaps humanity ridden with dented pride, frustration and envy has been unable to recognise or acknowledge these feats of incredible genius when first seen - or rather perhaps there is usually nowhere to go with the story - for the all-seeing eye sees all etc

Not in two minds today

The engineered? right/left schism in the human brain that prevents us being able to reproduce those high energy secular miracles ..

ROCK BRAIN AND FERTILE POLLEN AT THE SHERATON, EDINBURGH

.. or some might say in every Windows PC has an Intel chipset designed like an ancient Egyptian Temple. The CPU, BIOS Chip, RAM slots and Co-processor match up in proportion on the motherboard to the ancient Temple floorplan, even performing generally related preliminary functions - effectively turning PC users all over the globe into those 'switching on' an act of worship to the Egyptian pantheon. e.g. Perez notes that the motherboard has identical resonance with the floor-plan of the Temple of Horus at Edfu - completed in 57BC.
The site of the temple is also where Horus was said to have fought Seth. Along the walls are many inscription describing different battles and myths.

It does seem that those who have capacity to live off and recycle life energies and intentions for their own benefit did not just confine themselves to their underground *hi-tek* cities, but are happy to roll up their sleeves, pull on their wellies and muck-in on the organic free-range stress farm that is humanity.

image: cruel-looking sculpture in banking district, Edinburgh, Scotland.

ACADEMIC LAUNDRY

In the absence of more paranormal evidence and explanations, the establishment's academic 'driving engine of urban revolution' modelled by V G Childe, remains today one of the best and normal-sounding explanations for the western spread of toolmaking social organisations and civilisations from Mesopotomia. It tends to substantiate a constant driving ergonomic and painful application of bone and sinew against heavy rocks, usually not always an option that one could avoid in between tea breaks at the temple Quarry.

Whereas the 'Barsoom' science fiction series by Edgar Rice Burroughs which speaks of the adventures of John Carter of Mars, a cavalry officer from Virginia who was transported to Mars in the 19th Century and takes on the dark and occult reality engineers who 'manage the death of worlds, feasting on the distress' may be very close to the truth. However, it is to the more tangible 'Forbidden Archaeology' of Michael Cremo we can turn, to look for answers to the anomalies in the 'usual stories' of 'Egyptology' and the 'African' origins of mankind.

Given what we know of as 'human history' had to start somewhere and what we can see of it needs some explanation, then VG Childe's explanations of the process of mankinds social evolution are very plausible and basic without any need to resort to the 'high strangeness' of some of the 'other' artefacts and what their presence really means.

In fact all of this Ethnological data is simply what humanity remembers of the way they were - those 'elder gods' before the alleged fall of Atlantis.
All the alleged new 'civilised' ways are not some natural progression of mankind from some stone-age state.

e.g. why not evolve faster – war less, build, research and

develop and think more, tolerate less corruption etc In the 21st Century political excuses for the lack of human education, medicine, food, shelter and technology etc do not have a truthful or good financial/fiscal explanation.
Also the concepts of population reduction because the 'planet and its resource base' is 'unsustainable' are also a myth given the possibility of the global deployment of even non-esoteric [non-Tesla] water based engines.

As opposed to the large scale social adoption of the electrogravity engines of Townsend Brown. e.g. the black triangular TR3B e.g. these electrogravitic technologies if publicly available and democratically controlled could have supplied millennia of Utopia; purified the air, oceans, and waters, simplified clean factorial and food production and made living for innumerable people on earth sustainable indefinitely.

Fostering on Earth an unending social Utopia of soul growth and love. What's not to like about that ?

There is though, the sight of one very, very obvious and determined piece of social constructionism that with its empirical and scientific realism puts paid to any debate about who was doing what to whom and when and even how ....

The picture of a laser blaster lying on the sands of Mars - either placed there for human cameras or dropped in intense Interstellar combat ?

It did seem easier and less stressful to think of some clever Neanderthal persisting and 'getting ahead' etc but then *homosapiens* would seem to be recently re-inventing the wheel ! Note that the crashed starships and space-age rubble on Mars predates Humanity on Earth.

SEEMS CHILDEISH ?

Childe's 'urban revolution' is a monocausal theory of city emergence. This theory places the onus on technology, described as the 'engine of historical change', as the only significant factor in the emergence of cities.

Doing 'human academia' as an explanatory force for good though couldn't find it really explaining much about these incredibly well done very ancient cities built by 'perfect' megalithic builders who seemingly could carve very hard massive rocks using only smaller hard rocks they found lying about etc.

Whereas Childe understood the establishment of cities during an urban revolution to be driven by the momentum of technological innovations (e.g. in particular metallurgy) dating from the Neolithic Age (ca. 9000 B.C.) onwards it was actually a more 'starwars' explanation that really fitted all the facts.

Accordingly, the period of urban 'revolution' from the Neolithic age can be said to have taken place over several thousand years (i.e. 9000 B.C.. to approximately 3500 B.C..). Thus, although this can be called a 'revolution' in a broader sense, in that technology changed the face of society, it was allegedly through the intelligent adaptation by human society over time, to its emergent needs within variable environments, that these technologies arose.

None of that thinking though explained what happened to the Vimanas, the airships floating without gravity in India, or going round melting the rock walls of fortresses or dopping, by some accounts, nuclear weapons.

Nor could the theories of Childe explain what happened on Mars to an obviously highly evolved civilisation in similar circumstances and 'management'.

Suppose though, through these epochs of determined 'social constructionism' of humanity - despite a secret and hidden third factor here not picked up on or mentioned anywhere - i.e. despite 'organic distress farming' by a telepathic species specialised in the regulation and milking of human intentions - the souls of humanity with their usually robust connection to God, the Source of all life persist through the artificial 'deconstruction and desolation' of their good human intentions.

Childe's 'technological determinism' appears simple because it suggests that once scientific and technological ideas and processes are identified as good ideas, then presumes, devoid of 'occult' factors, that they would automatically be adopted by a society quite independent of any social, political or religious interests, in other words, that these ideas are 'autonomous'.

Thus, although the social constructionists better explain the extent and breadth to which cities developed in the ancient Near East once the diffusion of Mesopotamia's technologies were in place. Childe's theory, on the other hand, explains how these disseminating influences arose in the first place in the primarily hydraulic society of Mesopotamia - it is to the antithesis of these factors we must turn for clarity.

Given human beings have a reliable, creative soul-based, reasonable and end-based drive to extend and invest in and develop the reality they can see - outpouring into and causing great works of change and growth - then theories of 'social constructionism' and 'social determinism' seem to explain some of what can be historically seen.

What has not been picked up on - probably because of its 'occult' nature is a countervailing process simultaneously underway from a different species to humanity.

That is the soul farming counter-song - an engineered social 'deconstructionism' by non-human managers of desolation: - 'social nihilism'.

These non-human progeny utilise human 'dairy farming' that milks and harvests the soul-energies of distress.

e.g. 100 years of combustion engines and dire rhetoric of unsustainable lives and global destruction despite clean technological alternatives in the 21st Century.

The activities of a 'Hidden Hand' that intervenes and steers human history is a recurring complaint amongst hard done by humans.

One may find reference to it in modern conspiracy legends and myths penned by e.g. Trevor Ravenscroft in his 'Spear of Destiny', or Roberts and Gilbertson's 'The Dark Gods', however, merely recycling historical rumour – often within the context of self-referential non-academic bibliographies is ultimately fruitless.
Having operated as an Ethnologist within the conspiracy community and having studied numerous amazing and difficult to substantiate events, it is refreshing to find that had I merely continued with a standard academic education at the UK's OPEN UNIVERSITY, I would have discovered what the academics already knew – there's nothing as strange as History.
OU COURSE AT308 provided two textbooks on 'Pre-industrial Cities and Technologies' edited by Chant and Goodman, 1999 A.D..

From these various academic works, the editors drew upon the efforts of Social historians, Technologists, Archaeologists and other Scientists to assemble a History of Technology.
The three examples cited here in this paper however, disown the other academic comment and course material supplied and deployed around these textbooks in other pamphlets etc as content intended to emphasise the Open Universities' own distinctive agenda in the social sciences as opposed to some other UK Universities specialist leanings in e.g. Philosophy, which can compete in the same scientific publications market for shelf-room in bookshops.
The two course textbooks on 'Pre-industrial Cities and Technology' are definitive and sufficient enough to supply all the material that I needed to write very good course essays with.
Any material quoted is representative of the ideologies that are said therein by this teaching University to give shape and form to the dilemmas of history that retarded the evolution of science and technology on this planet.
This very popular Open University Course AT308 has been very thoroughly researched and discussed and has retained its rigor-

ous framework for technological evolution on this planet throughout the 2001 A.D. deployment of the contradictory and refutational archaeological data of Michael Cremo, in his startling publication 'The hidden history of the Human Race.'
This amazing compilation of archaeological finds presented without spin and with recourse to professional scientific method could not have left even the subscribers to Charles Fort with a sceptical overview of history. Although Charles Fort's collection of strange paranormal absurdities as witnessed can be dismissed as relative hear-say, the archaeological finds as presented by Cremo were thoroughly researched by the professional scientists who found them and carry the weight of scientific legitimacy and falsifiability.
The Open University does pay attention to such developments. Recent AT308 Course updates in 2003 A.D. included the finding of a very large submersed agricultural settlement in the Indian Ocean. The alleged contradiction it provided to the paradigm supplied by V G Childe's theory of 'urban revolution' – an expansion driven along a militaristic infrastructure from the Tigris and Euphrates basin, propagated by the continuity of trade and ideologies was dismissed.
Although the submerged buildings in the Indian Ocean were numerous and ordered, seasonal cultivation and pastoral needs did not particularly endear a fixed locality to inhabitants in need of food and water throughout the entire year in ancient times. This could also be deduced from the presence of tartan amongst red-haired mummies in Dolmens in northern China. People were prepared to 'shop around' for a good meal and beverage and place to chill in those days.

The alleged city in the Indian ocean was downgraded by the OU to a mere agricultural settlement as the morphology of the settlement and therefore its implied functions, as deduced from the oceanographic scans did not immediately confer upon it the status of a specialised and diverse place of; trade, skills, manufacture and habitation. Presumably the restaurant and

shipwright signage was a bit barnacled.
Open University Course AT308, therefore, is a source of technological history that can be defined as a tool for upwardly mobile education that is both stable, and able – a definition in common with the cruise-liner 'Titanic'.

The three examples of academic breakage that illustrate an insufficiency in scientific reason to account for the total failure of reality come from 3 continents and civilised epochs.

1. CHINA
2. EUROPE
3. SOUTH AMERICA

1. The slow boat from China.

China, from around the time that the Huns, Goths etc were finishing off Rome circa 500 A.D. although also experiencing the wrath of Kublai Khan in the north of China – began a tangential approach to Civilisation that incorporated a more spiritual cosmology within the approach of civilised values to community and society.
Drawing also on Indian mathematics and astrological expertise, many important cultural exchanges took place between India and China that included the import of; architectural idiom, gunpowder components such as saltpetre, decimalisation and absolute zero.
[Chant and Goodman 1999, p. 271]
India therefore, was an important supplier of religious values, images and ideas, of opulent religious ideologies, ostentatious displays of wealth and empire. i.e. a good place to borrow some gold from in the event of a crisis.
The industrialisation of China was fraught with destructive and recurring rebellion and war, but in the main, the vast country of 4.3 million square miles was well served by extensive use of river and canal navigation and a very large stock of boats and ships over a period of 1500 years from 500 A.D.

Frequent wars amongst warlords with the resources and aspirations to build and rebuild and relocate huge capital cities would have created a frequent need to replenish treasure stocks for mercenary campaigns and the industries needed to supply them.

Although it could be said that the 'silk road' an 8000 kilometre road running from Chang' an in west China to Baghdad and Persia through the central Asian city of Samarakand through the Gobi desert in northern Tibet was the domain of the Mongol Hordes and blocked the opportunity to trade in the Mediterranean by overland commerce, the same could not be said of the far easier journey south around the Malaysian Peninsula and into the Indian ocean.

Consider that from the comfort of one's own expeditionary fleet, and borne south by favourable currents and winds, there would be no absence of supplies such as fresh water on the far shorter route to the places of known treasure.

It is strange therefore to consider that from e.g. the Sui and Tang Dynasties circa 479 A.D. right up to the Ming and Ch'ing Dynasties circa 1840 A.D. that this in fact, did not happen.

It may be that various aspects of the bad things from the east intimidated the ancient warlords of China e.g. Jesuit priests, Marco Polo (1271-1295 A.D.), or the Black Death 1347 A.D. but that the origins of rich Indian treasure would not have escaped any well organised imperialist of those eras.

Whilst the Emperor Yong Le, in the early 15th century sent naval expeditions into the Indian Ocean to trade with India and explore east Africa, warmongering was rather restricted presumably because of the possibility of an Indian alliance with Mongols.

The practise of even politically correct Emperors and warlords outsourcing new resources stopped around 1433 A.D..

[Chant and Goodman 1999, p. 289] relate, however, that ' some civil servants .. disgusted by alien .. government, withdrew from public life.' [Chant and Goodman 1999, p. 291] continue by saying that 'Historians have documented new Mongol threats from the north and steep increases in the cost of timber needed for shipbuilding to explain the end of naval exploration. They have noted political infighting associated with relocation of the capital...' 'It is hard to escape the view, however, that something deeper than politics and the price of timber was at issue. For the governing class to turn its back so abruptly on the rest of the world, and also to lose interest in science and mathematics, suggests a shift in values and a defensive, unadventurous outlook.'

[Chant and Goodman 1999, p. 282] The Chinese navy, founded in 1132 A.D., had sailing ships and also paddle-powered and sail-less top armoured attack craft that could travel and manoeuvre independent of wind direction and also move in reverse. All naval vessels were equipped to catapult gunpowder bombs into the enemy. Cannonade were also in use against the Mongol hordes as early as the 12th and 13th centuries and would also have been available for military ships.
Although the Chinese navy failed the stop the 18th and 19th century European expeditions from e.g. the Dutch East India Company and then the English East India Company, there appears to be no reason whatsoever for the superior Chinese navy not to have over-ran the Indian Ocean, the Persian Gulf and the continent of Africa in its quest for the resources that could keep the empire defended, or some warlord in a mercenary campaign in the intervening 600 years after the founding of the navy and the recognition of its uses.
The only academic explanation for the non-conquest and non-exploitation of the Indian ocean, the Arabian gulf and East Africa offered by leading academics is of a 'defensive and unadventurous' outlook to which [Mr Regis Huc in Chant C, 1999, p. 216] would add .. 'patient and resigned shopkeeper mentality.'

The Chinese (warlords) in their quest for the gold and treasure etc that would fuel their ambitions of conquest, conspiracy and defence never thought about the possibilities for conquest using the abundant surplus of shipping and the proven expertise available to use it.
The non-use of a proven resource base in India over a period of 700 years for the financing of huge mercenary campaigns e.g. against the Tartar and Mongol hordes, or White Lotus rebellion, because a gold hungry warlord was too lazy to send one of many thousands of ships from this vast continent to re-explore the proven treasure centres of India is ludicrous.

2. 'A Horse, a horse, my Kingdom for a Horse ...' [Shakespeare W, King Richard III, Act 5 Scene 4.]

From ancient Sumer c.a. 3500 B.C., it took 4000 years into Europe to discover how to harness a horse for heavy loads and heavy plough by adapting an ox harness.

Getting a new take on the yoke harness used for Oxen such that a collar harness could be attached to another draft animal with less muscles in front of the windpipe appeared to be impossibly hard.
The sort of difficult discovery civilisation makes once it starts using hot drinks in the cold jars it used to drink from.
Taking 4000 years to get a handle on a horse and how it breathes, however is a bit of a stretch of credibility.
The excuse of 'unfamiliarity with horse anatomy' by Burford doesn't wear in any of those war zones whatsoever.
The introduction of the heavy plough in northern Europe in the 10th century A.D. created the agricultural surplus necessary for the beginnings of; trade, specialisation and urban revolution that became the European Renaissance in the 15th century.
This inability to comprehend a horse over 4000 years delayed intensive cultivation and intensive social and scientific urbanisation, industrialisation and scientific invention by at least 400 years in Middle Ages Europe.
It was approximately 400 years after the introduction of the use of draft horses on the heavy plough that the Renaissance took place in Europe. [Burford A, in Chant 1999 page 29] and [White L, in Chant 1999, p 99].

Warring nobles, Goths, Huns, Mongols, Kings, Queens etc from about the time of the fall of Rome c.a. 500 A.D. would have been requiring supplies and heavy transport to conduct their campaigns often in the most difficult of terrain that could not always be accessed by porter or river transport. In the absence of Oxen, siege engines such as; ballista, rams, trebuchets etc and other applications of woodland for military use would have needed use of much of the spare horses from the numerous fallen in those battles.
500 years of stupidity before someone effectively straps up a horse doesn't seem credible.
Campaign after campaign, army after army, necessity after necessity, battle after battle, retreat after retreat, sagacious inves-

tigation of supply logistics from everyone who has ever seen, eaten, butchered, harnessed, shod, ridden and or collided with a horse later, and in 500 years cannot devise a contraption to allow it to pull a heavy load without choking.

A bit much considering scorched earth warfare between petty nobles and highly organised armies probably required burger king ox steak cuisine and an overwhelming need to get half a ton of arrows etc. to point B from whatever stronghold it was required to over-winter in.

Regardless of who ate the local Oxen, with hundreds of years of recurrent necessity in anarchic Eurasia [e.g. 600 A.D. – 1400 A.D.], and always plenty of unoccupied medium cavalry horses to use, in tens of thousands of combat dilemmas the military hierarchy were totally unable to harness a horse to a cart without strangling it or to invent a better harness to solve matters of large scale life and death than the Ox harness used in ancient Sumer and Rome.

There were 20th century schools of military thought that suggested that war was a driving factor in the evolution of human industry, and would cite the benefits of the cold war and the nuclear arms race as an influential factor in e.g. the electronics industry.

The arms race in the 20th century also became the space race and the subsequent development of super-light and super-tough alloys, plastics and fabrics and the process of miniaturisation could be seen to bring household benefits in; television technology, cold weather gear etc.

That however, does not take it away from the middle ages of Europe and their own early modern ways of thinking.

Burford in Chant 1999, p36, relates that oxen were sufficient for Rome, but had clearly forgotten that it was the sight of massed horseman using short composite horse bow that had seared its way across the static impediments to warfare created by Roman thinking all over northern Eurasia.

From then on, efficient mobilisation of arms and resources would be the best response to such threats, as hard-hitting light

cavalry could get everywhere at short notice.
Whereas the era of the beef burger drive thru had clearly commenced – people in the dark ages clearly knew what a horse was and how it could be variously used.

3. Getting stoned in South America.

The sites and structures of the ancient Mayan civilisation in South America are impressive indeed. As are the number of new age beliefs attributed to the accuracy of sunspot predictions, the mathematics of Mayan chaos theory and other aspects of astronomy and science that seem to show, according to irrational 'hippy' beliefs, a penchant for design that would have got them all jobs with the George Lucas Star wars films at Hollywood.
Much as I rather empathise with the sentiment of such imagery of perhaps a golden bee that looks like an aerodynamic 20th century jet fighter in a 'Von Daniken' book – the very thought that petroleum engines and considerations of atmospheric friction appeared to be touted as evidence of space faring beliefs, enabled me to ignore those crystal skulls and other such at least for the time being until I could discover what it was that the population of the Mayan Empire actually did for a living.
The impractical new age of the 20th century never actually did any meaningful work and seemed to assume that neither did their spaced out space brother counterparts from ancient but spacey south America.
Myself, obviously being more of a practical sort, reckoned that such a magnificent achievement as building walls on those mountainsides that had polygonal 50 - 100 tonne blocks with angular sides that could have made a very challenging xmas party game by ronco toys – would have been hard even with the tools, metals and technologies available to the concurrent pyramid and temple builders of; Mesopotamia, Egypt, Greece and Rome.
To assemble the; geometric, asymmetric, many sided, irregular,

shapes and forms from which those massive walls at Cuzco and Sacsahuaman were made would take; cutting tools, hoists, ramps, pulleys, metal smelting and mining and a mathematical precision of such finesse that even today in the 3rd millennium of humanity on this planets surface, one still could not insert a razor blade between them.

Had I only but known - for the hardest edged tools that the Mayans possessed was allegedly obsidian – a volcanic glass that could be splintered to cut meat and textiles, and, the bronze Aztec blades later used against Cortez, the conquistador.

Neither bronze or obsidian are hard enough to provide an impact on the metamorphic volcanic rocks of the Andes mountain chain – and whereas there may be local and regional variation within the static and drift geology, no skills within the construction industry were cited in Chant and Goodman 1999, pps. 242-251 as being able to make the tools that could cut those rocks to such precise geometric shapes. Muscle power and earthen ramps by default were cited as the cause of these incredible and massive and precise and ornate structures.

Worse still, it was with the utmost horror that I came to a shuddering stop at p. 251 of Chant and Goodman 1999.

I can only quote verbatim what I saw there .....

'There are strong similarities to the Egyptian pyramids. Like the Pharaohs, the Incas imposed a system of compulsory labour on tens of thousands of captives. They hauled huge boulders from quarries as in ancient Egypt, used log rollers, inclined planes and bronze crowbars to move them. The precise shaping and fitting is thought to have been achieved by the constant pounding of boulders by harder stones, a continuous action maintained by a force of thousands of labourers working in shifts' (Gasparini and Margioles, 1980, p324: Hardoy, 1973. p.465.)

I can buy the quarry stuff where-by banging wedges into sandstone and limestone in e.g. Egypt one could isolate and dislocate a large rough hewn boulder for subsequent refinement

and roll it away on rollers etc and haul it up a ramp. Also the geology of the Andean mountain chain, although predominately Igneous and metamorphic rock suggests that there was plenty of available materials to use of roughly equivalent hardness to make both tools and building materials out of.
However the organisation required to pound these massive and hard boulders into the precise polygonal shapes we today see as precisely fitting would have taken immense effort by the use of skills even if most of the civilian population worked along side the captives. [e.g. as in the Chinese canal system upgrade near 9th century Tang Dynasty, Chang' an]

Give the hand tools used were of roughly equivalent hardness or even harder than the boulders, the rocks themselves would be in constant use and not much more than another factor of 10 or 20 % harder than the construction material. Not being diamonds, they would need constant replacement too if used ceaselessly by thousands and thousands of labourers, skilled and unskilled.
Given that there was no substance harder than this cutting tool and that the cutting tool was an arbitrary shaped rock of useful size, shape and weight for use in this sort of construction, it would mean that the supervisors on these projects would need a relative army of tool searchers to acquire tools of the right size and weight.
As the local stone tools got used up, gradually, the search would have to widen to keep an army of thousands and thousands of workers working efficiently in shifts and moderately supplied with food and water.
Not every stone found that was hard enough could be of use to deliver efficient craftsmanship
The logistics of such an undertaking beggar belief. If the handtools sourced were too soft or too heavy or too bulky, then the project
would slow down and the labour force would expire.
I am aware of the Scottish saying that 'a bad workman always

blames his tools' but then at the same time – not everyone was born to cut surfaces in rock like they were brain surgeons. Perhaps it was the jealous cynic in me – but that's a lot of guys standing around with a sore arm for days on end being unable to eat. I suppose that they would not come to any 'arm. However, the crème de la crème of anaemic academic investigation still sticks with the heavy rock theory instead of taking the light sabre approach for the 21st century.

In conclusion it is my belief that the human academic paradigm cannot adequately (or willingly) explain or account for the distribution and assets of ancient civilisation on this planets surface.

image: the Pentagon building with a new, more-white stone section. (above author) Taken from the 'memorial garden' where hijackers were said to skillfully crash a large jet aircraft, leaving very little aircraft debris.

TO TEMPORARILY CONCLUDE

I was watching the Ridley Scott epic on Moses the other day and a number of things seemed to become clearer to me.

(Not that I agree with Scott's portrayal of the One True God as a petulant child.)

It's that there are about 5.5 Billion people on this planet today in the 21st Century who would actually envy the state of supply of the Israelite captives as portrayed in 1500 BC Egypt in their having bowls of food, shelter, water, clothing and warmth.

That after many Millennia of evolutionary carrot and stick, the Human race i.e. the race of Adam, have en-masse (Greater than 66%) failed to do much else than be victims of attrition caused by evil forces in this Earth-plane.

Certainly, in approximately 2 Billion of a 7 Billion Global population there appears to be a network of Technocrats doing the bidding of strange and bad Plutocrats who in devil-like manner seem to be negating every aspect of what has often appeared good e.gs. the goodness of nuclear family, the 'focus' of a disciplined childhood education, an age of consent geared to capable, post-puberty bodies and biology, a notion of religion tied in to harmless non-carnal love, the idea of food being nutritious and of medicine that treats causes not symptoms.

In this sparse, social 'scab of technology' with advanced infrastructure, factories, intensive agriculture and highly toxic modus operandii lurk devil-like predators - some of whom may have even deceived a self-appointed elect into thinking that they and their delegated servants could breakaway and start afresh in a metallic network of computerised caves whilst wearing metallic looking jump-suits.

Yet underpinning this alleged telic-looking (end-based) meander to some alleged hi-tek future in which we can apparently look forward to climbing into tin cans and diving down wormholes or switching on electrogravity to get between local planets and trekking to stars - is the certainty that it does seem to be a hoax.

The pattern is similar as far as early technocratic evolution is concerned - for example it took 500 years after Rome for western europe to adapt an ox-harness to facilitate the intensive agriculture from heavy horses that could enable technological and social specialisms of tools in various social niches. Because oxen were sufficient for Rome ! [A Burford]

Half a millennia !!

Then came the mechanics of steam and the 'Steam Punk' visions of accomplished-looking mechanisms and shortly after that there followed the electronic replication and duplication and transmission and production of data objects and of data - this was supposed to herald a Golden Age for Earth in the 20th Century - we all know it didn't.

In the 21st Century only about 10-15% of 7 Billion people can really benefit from some of these technological processes as a life changing medium.
And now over a Century after Tesla - there is still no way to supply the masses - the billions, with energy derived freely from

the environment the way Tesla had experimentally illustrated.

Cue therefore the global purges and massive population reduction outlined in the UN Agenda 21.

With the deliberate denial of the deployment of free-er energy by the elites we are collectively asked to live a lie of ' global unsustainability' to justify epic attrition to the masses that takes on a biblical and epic scale.
Instead in the 21st Century the older amongst us see the Hollywood-created aspirations and expectations of Sci-Fi Utopia get mellowed down and made to dissipate in front of our ageing eyes.

No longer in the UK for example can the young - associate the phonetics of the name 'Mr Spock' - the friendly, logical alien from StarTrek whose applications to science could enable us to manufacture human society at the next, interstellar, level. Instead Spock or something sounding very very similar is now a frivolous boot-sale App.

Similarly instead of the legacy of Nikola Tesla being about electrogravity-floating, gravity-defying cars [1904] and ships, and free, environmental energy, it has thanks to billionaire Elon Musk [2014] - become merely about some OK-performing conventional (expensive) electric cars and some stupid-looking wrestling robots built out of old gaming Atari interfaces.

Certainly no 'Star Trek the Next Generation' humanesque executive, autonomous super-robot called 'Data' - despite the 'rock star' staging and adulation for those that build these grunt 'Musk-bots'.

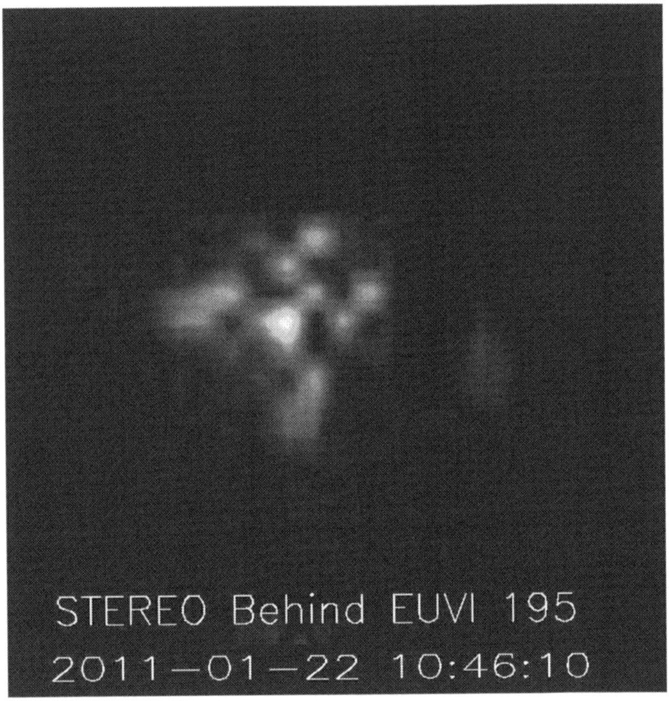

Images: UFO's in space from the NASA and JPL Soho Stereo Sun-cameras - e.g. aliens don't appear to be troubled by 'bedroom Atari programmers' !

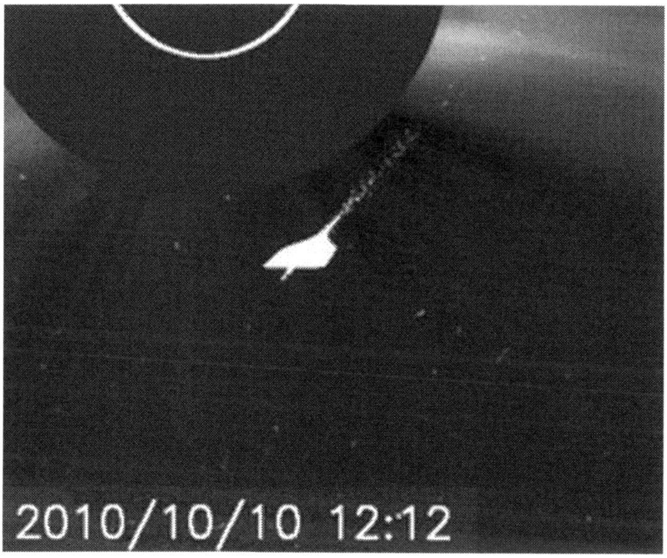

Future shock

We all know of the sub-surface break away Civilisation and that within the 15% benefiting from this probably about 15% of those are joining elite space navies and making the grade for colonial status or exotic robotics research, and we know that for all of mankind that's left - the masses, there is only a crippled vision of machine 'thinking' ability entrenched and handicapped by the Halting Problem. [Turing]

But with the 20th Century aspirations for the 21st Century now being trashed before the eyes of the people in the 'technosphere' who can recognise this - what is technocratic evolution really about ??

In with the bio-logical bricks ?

To the ever-enquiring young - possibly games and life and even travel in virtual reality, free from the constrictions of parental-type authority who want them to conform and 'be good' etc is where it is at.

Not acquiring 'property' but 'experiences' for their socially nurtured sense of self.

Every human, according to Descartes is willing to express two contradictory tendencies : to express themselves, and to disappear in something greater. Those tendencies, he suggests, lead to an error in development : we create collectives that are based on the oppression of some individuals and on the inflated ego of others.

This is for Behavioral Psychologist Koestler an error of transcendence that is reflected in a poor integration of our reptilian brain and cognitive brain !

The reptilian brain, according to a classic theory of brain science, has corresponding structures in the brains of mammals, including humans - allowing for thought, emotion and self-awareness.

In the 1960's, Neoroscientist MacLean's theory of the basal ganglia, which he called the reptilian brain, showed control of baser instincts such as aggression and territoriality, behavior that can be observed in reptiles as well as mammals, including humans.

Plenty 'medical' excuses therefore for those who choose to be programmed to socially fail.
With even the music of the 21st Century becoming non-melodic and often illiterate, angry rants to the sound of a machine, and with absolutely everyone being able to access and afford industry standard tools and media platforms - the new standards of excellence are to be found not in originality and creative thinking but in the actual and relative excellence of what the

tools and software do.
The new breed of artistes tend to 'produce' by formulaic processes and gadgets rather than create from the heart.

Contrast the disorientation of current youth with the disorientation of public science.

The theatrical staging at NASA though puts on some of the most expensive, loud, fireworks displays ever seen, utilising a technology first developed during the second world war. (mid 20th Century)

NASA meantime are most likely aware that antigravity is not 'rocket science' - yet persist with obsolete solid fuel internal combustion rockets. Meanwhile, even the Virgin Space corporation, were it not for inexplicable accidents and delays, could and should easily find themselves in Space but are not.

image: Nikola Tesla c.a. 1910

Our endless, warring poverty and captivity appears to be engineered and zoned by dark forces. Perhaps the Devil's greatest lie is that he does not exist !

The pantomime of this technology and its obvious nonsensical failures are happening to only a small percentage of the planets population for it's as if the Pharoahs of Old were still investing in pyramid hierarchies and 90% of their servants were still more than happy with sack cloth, mudhuts, some water from the Nile and a modest bowl of food.

Globally, for the huge majority in the last 4000 years nothing much has changed.

I can hear the objections to that statement already though - but .. '..we have science and medicine !' – e.g. how much, and how many Cancer cures does it take to cure Cancer ? (e.g. the very cheap and available Public domain molecule with no side-effects called DCA - or Di-Chloro Acetate).

What they would be referring to is a belief that by operating a scientific method by e.g. Karl Popper [1962], we could make great advances - but that's only a belief - as there is far too much inconvenient truth swept under the scientific carpet.

It's written down what to scientifically do ie the method - but then there are just so much other considerations of politics, cronyism and funding - that how the scientific truth is publically applied as an application is often an object of ridicule.

So, if life is not actually all about becoming Captain's; Kirk, Picard or Janeway what in fact is really going on on the Earth's surface ?

It's here that we enter a different realm - where aliens are soul-hungry interdimensional insectoid demons, operating only the appearance of technology; [Nigel Kerner - the Song of the Greys], having many names in many cultures - [e.g. elementals, demons, djinn, genius locii, greys, zeta reticulans, faeries, etc] and, where the shapeshifting Reptilians are fallen from Heaven and are devils, specialising in incarnations of life-hungry know-alls close to the edge of chaos. [Josephus Flavius - the History of the Jews].

The devil and its progeny also seem to use cultural aliases too e.g. [Nephilim, devils, Naga, Draco, Dragons, seelie court, High Elves, the HU, etc]

The reptilians incubating their progeny in whatever or whoever they can, appearing to manage and feast on the outpourings of the death of worlds as they travel down the decaying time stream. e.g. the abandoned pyramids and monuments of Mars.

We humans of the race of Adam have been easily distracted and herded over the ages with the pretender's superior abilities to access mind and life, faster than we can humanly process, beyond time space - to infest and invade our lives and dreams with desolate blasphemy.
That I think is the reason Christ came to us, to demonstrate the one truth that superceded every other – that in order to live eternally in peace somewhere wonderful – that by merely imitating osmosis in a vine, by imitating the giving and sharing of nature, we would naturally love and live forever.

We are going to need help to get home to Heaven it's true, but then traditionally that assistance has always been there when needed.

image: Archangel Michael slaying the dragon, Glenfinnan, Fort William, Scotland.

One day, c.a. 1884, According to Kevin Symonds, author of Pope Leo XIII and the Prayer to St. Michael, a vision likely occurred between 1884 and 1886 and took place during the celebration of Mass.

The aged Pope Leo XIII looking 'pale and fearful' suddenly sank to the floor in a faint. Attending Physicians who hastened to the scene could find no trace of his pulse and thought him dead.

However, after a short interval the Holy Father regained consciousness and exclaimed with great emotion:

"Oh, what a horrible picture I have been permitted to see!"

A cardinal at the time who knew the pope's private secretary explains that *"Pope Leo XIII truly had a vision of demonic spirits, who were gathering on the Eternal City (Rome)..."*
He had been shown a vision of evil spirits who had been released from Hell and their efforts to destroy the Church. But in the midst of the horror the archangel St. Michael appeared and cast Satan and his legions into the abyss of hell. Soon afterwards Pope Leo XIII composed the following prayer to Saint Michael, now used in exorcism and deliverances. This is the original version:
Prayer to St. Michael the Archangel

"O Glorious Prince of the heavenly host, St. Michael the Archangel, defend us in the battle and in the terrible warfare that we are waging against the principalities and powers, against the rulers of this world of darkness, against the evil spirits. Come to the aid of man, whom Almighty God created immortal, made in His own image and likeness, and redeemed at a great price from the tyranny of Satan.

"Fight this day the battle of the Lord, together with the holy angels, as already thou hast fought the leader of the proud angels, Lucifer, and his apostate host, who were powerless to resist thee, nor was there place for them any longer in Heaven. That cruel, ancient serpent, who is called the devil or Satan who seduces the whole world, was cast into the abyss with his angels.

Behold, this primeval enemy and slayer of men has taken courage. Transformed into an angel of light, he wanders about with all the multitude of wicked spirits, invading the earth in order to blot out the name of God and of His Christ, to seize upon, slay and cast into eternal perdition souls destined for the crown of eternal glory.

This wicked dragon pours out, as a most impure flood, the venom of his malice on men of depraved mind and corrupt heart, the spirit of lying, of impiety, of blasphemy, and the pestilent breath of impurity, and of every vice and iniquity.

"These most crafty enemies have filled and inebriated with gall and bitterness the Church, the spouse of the immaculate Lamb, and have laid impious hands on her most sacred possessions. In the Holy Place itself, where the See of Holy Peter and the Chair of Truth has been set up as the light of the world, they have raised the throne of their abominable impiety, with the iniquitous design that when the Pastor has been struck, the sheep may be scattered.

"Arise then, O invincible Prince, bring help against the attacks of the lost spirits to the people of God, and give them the victory. They venerate thee as their protector and patron; in thee holy Church glories as her defense against the malicious power of hell; to thee has God entrusted the souls of men to be established in heavenly beatitude. Oh, pray to the God of peace that He may put Satan under our feet, so far conquered that he may no longer be able to hold men in captivity and harm the Church. Offer our prayers in the sight of the Most High, so that they may quickly find mercy in the sight of the Lord; and vanquishing the dragon, the ancient serpent, who is the devil and Satan, do thou again make him captive in the abyss, that he may no longer seduce the nations.
O God, the Father of our Lord Jesus Christ, we call upon Thy holy Name, and as supplicants, we implore Thy clemency, that by the intercession of Mary, ever Virgin Immaculate and our Mother, and of the glorious St. Michael the Archangel, Thou wouldst deign to help us against Satan and all the other unclean spirits who wander about the world for the injury of the human race and the ruin of souls. Amen."

Roman Raccolta, July 23, 1898, supplement approved July 31, it was then abridged in 1902, in; London: Burnes, Oates & Washbourne Ltd., 1935, 12th edition.

Short Prayer to St. Michael the Archangel
The well-known short version of this prayer follows in English. The Pope ordered this prayer to be recited daily after Low Mass in all the churches throughout the Catholic world. However this practice was almost completely swept away in the 1960s by liturgical changes made in the wake of Vatican Council II. Co-incident with the Marian prophesies and missives from Fatima about the need for prayers for the Church!

Saint Michael the Archangel, defend us in battle,
be our protection against the malice and snares of the devil.
May God rebuke him we humbly pray; and do thou, O Prince of the Heavenly host, by the power of God, thrust into hell Satan and all evil spirits
who wander through the world for the ruin of souls.

Amen.

To conclude therefore - the serpent, and its progeny willingly choose to live in and create deceptions and falsehoods with which to ensnare the souls of the temporarily disadvantaged Race of Adam.
It might be that we cannot recognise or even see such things - and if I'm honest that isn't too bad because we can always plead stupidity when we eventually come to review our lives beyond Earth.
On the other hand though, merely becoming a beacon of occasional but persistent prayer and being able to persist with that way of being, in a loving, simple and gentle way, is going to cause the enemy temporal grief.
re: 'crushing the serpents of Eden underfoot etc

A footnote provided a couple of hundred years ago by Bishop Challoner, in his revision of the Douay-Rheims (Catholic Bible) version, state, re he or she crushing the 'serpents head' from:

Genesis 3:15 which says,

"I will put enmities between thee [the serpent] and the woman, and thy seed and her seed: she shall crush thy head, and thou shalt lie in wait for her heel."

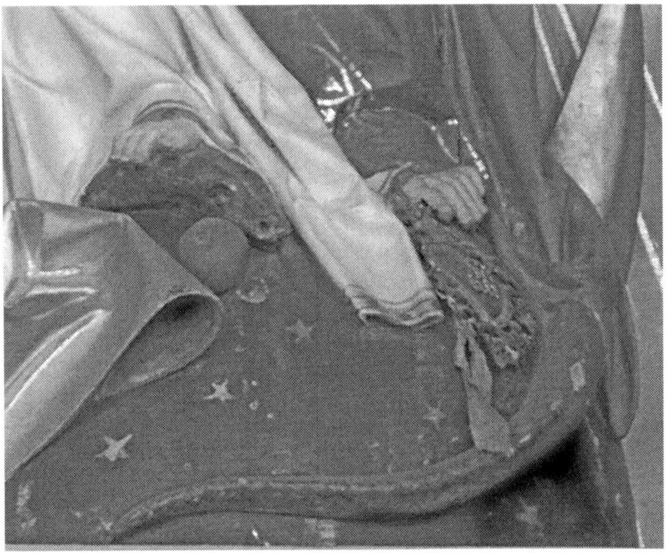

image: the foot of the Lusenburg Virgin.

Whether Greek or Hebrew or male or female language in translations etc *"The sense is the same: for it is by her seed, Jesus Christ, that the woman crushes the serpent's head."*
(A Catholic Commentary on Holy Scripture, Bernard Orchard, O.S.B., ed. [New York: Thomas Nelson and Sons, 1953], p. 186.)

So to conclude this work - evidence for the Serpents of Eden can be found almost everywhere, and although they appear superior in some things, this is only a temporary advantage over the sons and daughters of Adam and Eve.

It takes time to shake away the dusty vision of tin cans and engines in space, flashing panels and portals to endless medievalism - but then - once we can recognise the same issues in many different guises, and are finally able to look up from the spiritual treadmills - even the food with the most additives on Earth will lose its savour.

Whereas it took the majority of my own life on Earth to finally see the truth here, it was never the case that I was alone and without a prayer.

Andrew Hennessey.

Made in the USA
Columbia, SC
02 September 2022

66562942R00095